Contents

Beth MacEoin

Beth MacEoin trained at the Northern College of Homeopathic Medicine for four years before setting up her practice and becoming a registered member of the Society of Homeopaths. Beth has ten health books to her credit, acts as an advisor to journalists on many magazines and newspapers. She also broadcasts on BBC Radio Newcastle and has appeared several times on Tyne Tees television to give advice on general health topics.

Introduction

If you feel you don't have enough time to read this book, then it's been written especially with you in mind. So many of us have good intentions about getting to grips with a better time management plan, healthier diet, starting a new physical fitness regime or learning relaxation techniques. Often we put it off until some time in the future when we imagine we will have more time to embark on these positive changes.

The sobering news is that the best time to take stress management action is right now, since we are likely to have even less time in the future if we lead a high-stress lifestyle. However, if we make the positive decision to take action at this moment we will reap all of the positive benefits sooner and feel the delightful sense of accomplishment that comes with changing the quality of our lives for the better.

The contents of this book have been deliberately organized in such a way that we will easily find the best way for us to make the changes that we will most benefit from. Some of us may want to read the text from cover to cover, while others may instinctively feel drawn towards the sections that have the most relevance for them. How each person chooses to use the information that is given in the following pages is up to them, since the flexibility of the content allows for this sort of creative use. Once the first big step of deciding to take action has been made, the rest should gradually fall into place.

The Stress Epidemic: Fact or Fiction?

Before we can feel committed to take action, we need to identify that there is a genuine problem in the first place. What can we make of the assertions that negative stress levels are reaching serious proportions, especially in the workplace? Is it a genuine problem with facts and figures to back it up, or is the whole concern about escalating stress levels, like lunch – strictly for wimps who just need to pull themselves together and get down to the task in hand?

Perhaps the best (and often most convincing) way of objectively assessing the degree of the problem is to have a cool look at the disruption and costs associated with stress-related claims at work to date. According to Professor Cary Cooper at the Manchester School of Management, in 2002 British employers had to respond to a record 164,000 claims for stress-related injury and illness at work. These figures were up by more than one-third of such claims for the previous year. It has been estimated that every day approximately 270,000 workers in the United Kingdom take time off due to stress, and that a staggering £7 billion each year is lost in lower production, sickness payments and NHS charges. As we can see, stress-related issues at work are generating attention as well as costing money, and so it makes a great deal of sense to accept that we do have an identifiable problem here that is not going to go away if we ignore it.

The Workplace as a Stress Magnet

Our jobs can be a blessing or a curse, depending on how much job satisfaction we obtain from what we do every day and how much stress we have to cope with on a daily basis. Below is a quick run-down of some of the most common reasons why negative stress levels can build within the workplace. Each of these issues will be dealt with in depth later in this book.

Financial Security

Although it's not the sole reason for working, most of us will assess new job prospects by balancing financial gain against general professional satisfaction. If it looks as though our job is under threat or insecure in any way, then this can create a great deal of negative stress, since we will know that the situation is beyond our immediate control. Feeling helpless in this way is one of the most powerful negative stress factors we can encounter.

Identity

If we don't have an active, satisfying quality of life outside of work, there is a strong chance that we may begin to feel that our basic identity is bound up with what we *do* rather than what we *are*. This may be fine in the short term (especially if we get a lot of job satisfaction from our professional life), but it can leave us open to a significant negative stress load if we begin to over-identify with the job we're involved in. This can escalate to especially difficult levels if we feel our job is under threat, or if we actually have to face redundancy or early retirement.

Physical Pressures

Even if we aren't involved in a job that is especially physical, we may be subject to subtle stresses at work that can result in rising mental tension and physical discomfort. This can involve anything such as being given faulty equipment to work with, having to work under inadequate lighting, or using a desk that's causing low-grade postural problems.

Pressure of Time

The amount of time we're allocated to do a task often determines whether we see it as a challenge or as a negative pressure. With workforces being trimmed so that business becomes more lean and cost-effective and targets being constantly increased, there's little wonder that many of us may begin to feel stressed out and tense when we're asked to meet seemingly impossible deadlines. In such a situation, learning the skill of effectively prioritizing tasks and maximum positive management of time can be a transforming experience (provided, of course, the targets being presented to us are achievable).

How This Book Can Help

We may not be able to change our working situation overnight into a more satisfactory or rewarding one, but the information contained within this book is designed to give some essential, effective, practical strategies. We can use these to help us deal more proactively with the unpleasant effects of negative stress on our minds and bodies.

Once we start using these simple but effective stress-busting measures on a daily basis, we are likely to experience a great number of benefits. These include greater mental clarity, increased capacity to focus on whatever task is at hand, enhanced motivational skills, more physical energy, and an ability to bounce back quickly from setbacks as they arise. As a result, we will be in a better position to evaluate how we feel about our jobs at a base-line level, once we're not bogged down by a host of stress-related symptoms. Bearing this in mind, freedom from negative stress is just a few essential steps away. Why not take the very first and move on to Chapter One? Your body is likely to thank you for it!

Chapter One

The Global Problem

If we are to get to grips with a working understanding of the huge subject of stress, it helps enormously to start with a simple explanation of what happens on a purely physical level when we go through a classic reaction to a stressful stimulus. Once we have established how and why this starts, and the way in which it leads to a predictable series of physical, mental and emotional reactions, we can begin to learn how to handle these reactions in a positive, proactive way.

Within this particular context, knowledge truly is power, since much of the distress that accompanies unmanaged stress is magnified by feeling powerless in the face of some disturbing physical symptoms, which often feel totally out of proportion to the situation. Once we have learnt some practical, basic tools for effectively turning down or switching off the stress response, we are likely to find that we feel empowered to tackle areas of our lives that we know need attention. Beforehand we may have felt we lacked the necessary confidence, drive, energy or focus to do anything about it. These areas of uneasiness could involve anything, such as getting down to a demanding project at work, initiating a new relationship, confronting the skills needed to give public presentations, or getting our finances finally in order. Although some of these don't happen within the workplace, they can raise our overall level of background stress, which can have knock-on effects that spill over into our professional lives. These may include lack of concentration, persistent fatigue, recurrent headaches or feeling generally jaded and lacking the 'edge' that we need if we are to perform well and decisively.

If every time we try to initiate any of these activities our bodies react as though we're about to face a sabre-tooth tiger, we are clearly going to be on a hiding to nothing as far as generating a successful outcome is concerned. However, if we start to understand why our bodies throw these uncomfortable, distracting and panic-inducing sensations at us during times of stress and pressure, we will be taking our first important steps on the path to effective stress management.

Stress Reactions: The 'Fight or Flight' Response

Whenever we encounter a severely stressful situation we can guarantee that a number of physical reactions are going to take place, which may include any combination of the following in varying degrees of severity:

- dry mouth
- nausea
- conciousness of a rapid heartbeat
- sweating
- stomach cramps and/or diarrhoea
- rapid, shallow breathing
- light-headedness.

In addition, we are likely to find that we feel a mounting sense of panic, with difficulty in mentally focusing or concentrating on any information that may be coming our way.

Without our conscious awareness, blood is pumped to our muscles in order to prepare them for flight, our adrenal glands secrete the stress hormone adrenaline, blood sugar levels rise to give us more energy to deal with whatever threat we're confronted with, while blood pressure is also raised.

All of these physical changes are automatically initiated when we feel stressed. It's all down to a primitive, instinctive response to danger, which is designed to help us retaliate or sprint away as quickly as possible. This is known as the 'fight or flight' response. Sadly, our nervous systems haven't caught up with the reality of the kind of stress we're most likely to encounter as a result of twenty-first-century living and working conditions, as an inappropriately, frequently-triggered fight or flight response can become a hindrance rather than a help in the health stakes. Common health problems that are known to arise as a result of, or become exaggerated by, a poorly-managed, overly-stressful working environment may include any combination of the following:

- insomnia
- hypertension (high blood pressure)
- fatigue
- poor concentration, mental performance and inability to focus
- anxiety
- depression
- tension headaches
- irritable bowel syndrome
- eczema
- psoriasis
- diminished appetite or compulsive comfort eating
- stomach ulcers
- chronic indigestion
- muscle aches, pains and/or trembling.

Before we learn practical skills and strategies for switching off the negative stress reactions that can lead to some of the unpleasant symptoms listed above, we need to take a bird's eye view of the autonomic nervous system. By doing so, we'll gain an understanding of how it's made up of two opposing branches that need to balance each other for optimum chance of stress management to occur.

The Sympathetic and Parasympathetic Nervous System

Although we're not consciously aware of it, the autonomic nervous system is implicated in an impressive array of wide-ranging bodily processes which can include triggering perspiration, stimulating digestive secretions, raising or lowering blood pressure, regulating heartbeat, and initiating physical changes that come about as a result of sexual arousal.

In order to be able to respond efficiently, the autonomic nervous system relies on the balanced functioning of its two opposing components, called the sympathetic and parasympathetic branches. When these two aspects work in harmony they provide us with an excellent example of how a perfect, balanced whole can be made up of two wings that have diametrically opposite functions.

The sympathetic branch is intimately bound up with the fight or flight response outlined above, due to its connection with adrenaline secretion. Once the sympathetic wing of our nervous system kicks into action, we experience an upsurge of nervous energy that prepares us to meet physical, emotional or mental pressure by accelerating the heartbeat, pumping extra blood to muscles, speeding up the breathing rate and shutting down the secretion of gastric juices. In other words, it's the job of the sympathetic nervous system to provide us with the necessary 'edge' that is needed in order to perform well under pressure.

This state of arousal is balanced by the parasympathetic wing of the nervous system. This is the branch of the autonomic nervous system that is responsible for helping us unwind and 'chill out' once we've (ideally successfully) met whatever pressure or challenge we've been faced with. So, as we can imagine, this part of the nervous system helps initiate totally opposite reactions to those triggered by the sympathetic branch. As a result, effective parasympathetic activity helps bring down blood pressure levels, slow down heartbeat, initiate smooth digestive functioning, and slow down respiration. In other words, it produces the sensations that are associated with feeling fully and deeply relaxed. Those of us who generally feel we can rise to challenges effectively and productively, but readily feel mentally, emotionally and physically relaxed within a short space of time, are likely to be enjoying balanced sympathetic and parasympathetic nervous system activity.

However, the good news is that even if we're not one of the lucky people who are able to do this instinctively, there are effective, practical skills that we can learn to switch on parasympathetic activity whenever we need to calm down and unwind. There are huge practical advantages to being able to do this effectively, since we're likely to find that, as concentration levels improve, stress-related symptoms have less of a chance to develop and distract us, and as a result we're going to feel generally much more focused and productive. Sadly, the reverse side of the coin (where the sympathetic wing of the nervous system is in a state of constant response) may make us feel 'wired up' and energized in the short term. The effect is a little like driving a car constantly in fifth gear regardless of the terrain. Not surprisingly, if this goes on for too long, a state of mental, emotional and physical burn-out is going to be lurking not too far down the road.

Ignoring the emergence of any combination of stress-related symptoms is very like ignoring warning lights that appear on the dashboard of a car, and we do so at our peril. They are there for a very good reason, since awareness of a growing problem and taking appropriate action to solve it is the only way of avoiding a more complicated (and possible threatening) problem further down the line.

So, if a significant proportion or combination of any of the following symptoms occur, it is time to take stock and turn the situation around. Not only is your body likely to thank you for it, but your boss and colleagues should do so too!

- Mood swings that move from 'highs' to 'lows' swiftly and without warning
- Reliance on increasing amounts of alcohol, cigarettes, and/or painkillers to cope
- Cravings for sweet, 'junk' foods
- Avoidance of tasks that need doing urgently
- Difficulty in prioritizing tasks
- Using sleeping tablets to mask an inability to switch off and rest at night
- Back pain
- Easily-triggered irritability and mental and emotional 'short fuse'
- Recurring minor infections that seem to move from one to another

Factors Likely to Trigger the Stress Response

As we have already discussed, there isn't much likelihood of the fight or flight response being triggered at work by the presence of a physical threat (unless we are rather daring in our choice of occupation and become a steeplejack or bomb disposal expert!). For most of us it's not a major physical crisis at work that trips the fight or flight reaction. It could be a series of strains and stresses that may each be fairly minor in itself but, when taken together, can be enough to make us feel a sense of jitteriness and edginess that is quite out of proportion to the situation.

Of course, one person's stress is another's stimulation, since each of us is likely to have our own individual physical and psychological make-up that responds in its own unique way to pressures and challenges. All of the following are common stress factors in the professional sphere that can get the best of us feeling tense and pressured, especially if they occur within the context of having a bad day.

Being Asked to Meet Unreasonable Targets or Deadlines
When we feel under pressure and yet more is being heaped upon us, it can prevent us from seeing the wood for the trees. In order to handle stress factors effectively, it really is very important to stand back and assess whether what we are being requested to do is achievable (although challenging) or downright impossible. Nothing is quite so stressful as feeling disempowered, so when something extra is being asked of us, we need either to empower ourselves by taking appropriate action (this in itself can be a great professional stress diffuser) or to find a compromise solution through positive communication.

Feeling Stuck in a Professional Rut
Being experienced at a job brings its rewards and compensations, but all of us need to guard against the boredom that can inevitably set in when an occupation becomes routine. Most of us know that too many tough challenges can overload us with stress, while some of us may be surprised to realize that boredom and apathy can also contribute to powerful feelings of being negatively stressed. In many occupations this sense of stagnation isn't given the time or space to happen, as there may be regular training opportunities on offer, combined with regular promotion prospects, or moving laterally into divergent aspects of the same profession over an extended period. If this isn't happening, it may be down to each of us to find ways of remaining stimulated by what we do: if this stops happening and interest refuses to be re-kindled, it could well be time to think about moving to a new job.

Poor Communication Skills
It helps to remember that communication needs to move effectively between both sides (employer and employee) for the most positive form of communication to take place. Ideally employers and those

in senior management need to ensure that an effective structure is put in place that allows communication to move down the chain of command as quickly and effectively as possible. Any strong feelings on the ground-floor level also need to be clearly and assertively expressed rather than nursing grievances. This is the ideal scenario but sadly many of us have to work within a framework that is less than ideal. However, there are still practical skills we can learn about becoming more effective communicators that will still do some good, even in the most difficult professional situation. We'll have a quick tour of some of these skills and learn how to acquire them in Chapter Three.

Poor Organizational Skills

Poor organizational skills can apply to everything, from the way we arrange our personal surroundings to time management. Some of us may have positive organizational and time management skills without having to give it a second thought, while others have to learn them. However much time and effort it may take to acquire these skills, it's worth every moment spent in taking the trouble to do so. Nothing is quite so likely to trigger the fight or flight response on a constant low-grade level than feeling surrounded by tasks that are building up around us. Feeling powerless to know where to start to take action is one of the foundation stones of a negative stress response, especially if this feeling is being reinforced by disorganized surroundings. However, starting to take positive action is immensely therapeutic as it rapidly makes us feel we are back in control again. What's more, always remember, it is never too late to start!

Low Morale at Work

Feeling stressed and tense can be extremely contagious among staff who work closely together, and if this continues for too long it can have a disastrous effect on general morale. Sadly, when problems exist higher up the job ladder and percolate downwards, there is unlikely to be a swift or easy answer to the problem. In situations like this it becomes more important than ever to find ways of diffusing your own stress levels and turning on the relaxation response. As a result, although you may not be able to change the overall motivational context that you work within, you are far less likely to get mentally, emotionally or physically burnt out if you are able to recharge your energy through effective stress-reduction techniques.

Inadequate Working Environments

Don't forget that stress doesn't just arise from psychological pressures, since it can also be aggravated by having to work within a setting that may unwittingly be contributing to stress-related symptoms. Some of these environmental stresses can be sparked off by a badly set up workstation that exaggerates postural tension and discomfort. Poor lighting is one of the most common triggers of recurrent headaches and fatigue around the eyes, as are noisy surroundings or lack of privacy when making important phone calls in an open-plan environment.

Most of these will be discussed in the next two chapters, along side practical suggestions about to simple ways of making our working surroundings as tension-free, or at least as stress-reduced, as possible.

Common Stress-related Body and Mind Symptoms

As we've seen in the sections earlier in this chapter, a negative stress response affects the whole body in a complex and profound way. Consequently, when we're dealing with stress factors in a proactive, dynamic way we are most likely going to feel energized, challenged and extremely positive as a result.

However, when we're in a negative stress reaction state, the very opposite is most likely to happen. As a result, those of us who are familiar with feeling negatively stressed may be no strangers to many of the common mental, emotional and physical symptoms listed below:

- inability to switch off when exhausted
- poor communication skills through feeling too rushed to explain things thoroughly
- lack of mental focus
- inability to prioritize
- poor memory

- lack of confidence
- anxiety for no particular reason
- mental and emotional 'short fuse' with a marked tendency to explode for the most minor of reasons
- tearfulness
- a sense of emotional detachment or flatness
- lack of sparkle
- roller-coasting energy levels with surges of energy rapidly followed by exhaustion; this applies as much to mental and emotional energy as it does to physical vitality
- fluttering in the chest
- migraines or constant headaches
- lowered or absent libido
- feeling sick
- complete lack of appetite or binges of comfort eating
- addictions (these can be fairly minor, such as cravings for sugar, caffeine, junk foods and cigarettes, or more disruptive, such as a serious dependency on alcohol and/or recreational drugs)
- physical twitchiness.

Chapter Two

Inside the Workplace

When we consider the huge proportion of our waking hours spent at work, it would be marvellous to live an ideal world where we all feel fulfilled, secure, appreciated and content as we go about our daily tasks. Sadly, this is not the reality for the majority of us who feel pressured, frustrated, anxious, unfulfilled and disgruntled about the working conditions that we may have to put up with on a daily basis.

What follows in the next two chapters sadly cannot act as a magic wand to provide us with the perfect job and working conditions at a single stroke – if only this were possible! But they do give some very practical advice that we can apply in whatever way we choose to improve our working experience. How we decide to use this information will, of course, be applied by each of us in a different way, appropriate to our individual working stresses. However, care has been taken when considering these issues to make sure that they have a general significance, so that most of the concerns explored below will have equal significance to us if we are part of an organized workforce or whether we are self-employed.

Since common areas of negative stress exert their draining influence on us whatever the reality of our working environment, it is the purpose of this chapter to highlight where these flashpoints lie so that positive action can be taken to ease the situation.

Where do the Workplace Stress Flashpoints Lie?

Here we will be exploring the areas that are most commonly triggers for negative stress. This does not attempt to be an exhaustive run-down of all of the potential triggers of negative pressure and tension in the workplace, but it does attempt to guide us in the right direction so that we may go on to identify areas that apply to our own work environment.

Working Hours and Timescales

Time is something that can cause huge negative stress problems. Deadlines, however demanding, always need to be ultimately achievable; otherwise, when pushed to work within an unreasonable timeframe, we will become increasingly stressed as we see our deadline looming closer and the work nowhere near completion.

Absence of Regular Breaks

Keeping on working through breaks and lunch hours is one of the most counterproductive stress management strategies we can employ. Initially seductive because we seem to be saving time in the short term, the long-term effect is almost certainly going to promote escalating, rather than reduced, stress levels. Skipping regular breaks has counterproductive effects on emotional equilibrium, mental health and physical well-being, as we shall see in Chapter Three and especially in Chapter Six.

Putting Off Unpleasant or Boring Tasks

Procrastination is one of the single most likely factors at work to most trigger or maintain unhealthy, escalating stress levels. We might think we are cutting ourselves some positive psychological slack when we put things that need to be done on to a mental back-burner, but sadly the reverse is true. Even if this knowledge is lurking at a non-conscious level, it is enough to make us feel stressed and uneasy. Fortunately, the exhilaration and sense of relief that comes with finally getting down to what needs to be done is proportionally large.

Lack of Resources

In order to do any job most effectively and satisfyingly, we need to feel confident that we have the essential support we need to accomplish the task in hand, otherwise we risk being sabotaged in one way or another. Whenever you find any professional task an uphill struggle, it is always worth stopping for few minutes to mentally stand back and trying as objectively as possible to assess whether this situation has crept up without your realizing it. Also don't forget to consider this issue from as creative a perspective as possible. For instance, lack of appropriate resources could involve adequate manpower, realistic timeframes, basic information, working materials or ongoing professional training and development.

A 'Sick' Working Environment

If we are really engrossed in the professional task at hand, it is ever so easy to ignore aspects of our immediate surroundings that may be less than healthy. If you need to take time off in order to recuperate from recurrent minor infections such as a regular colds or sinusitis, consider whether the air conditioning and central heating systems are working in an efficient or balanced way. Problems associated with 'sick building syndrome' will be discussed in the section at the end of this chapter.

Internal Stressors

In this section we consider some of the 'mind games' that can also be the focus of stress at work. In many ways, these can be some of the most challenging pressures to deal with, since they are often so subtle and develop in such an insidious way that we may not even recognize that they are a problem until they've built up to an intolerable level. Even more worryingly, we may give ourselves an unbearably hard time by automatically assuming that the problem must lie with us. While sometimes this may actually be the case, in many of the negative situations discussed below our sense of self-esteem and basic confidence may become so ground down over time that we automatically see ourselves and our capabilities in a negative light.

Competitiveness

A certain amount of healthy competition can give us the impetus and 'edge' that we may need to keep focused and productive. After all, if all signs of competition were somehow magically removed from our lives, there is a very good chance that a certain degree of motivation would also disappear. The trick to maintaining a healthy level of competition is to make sure that it remains balanced. When this is the case, allowances must be made for things to go slightly off track now and again, so that a slight glitch in achievement isn't allowed to loom large as a failure. We also need to ensure that competitiveness between ourselves and our colleagues doesn't spill over into 'dirty' tactics that deliberately undermine another's performance in order to ensure winning. This tends to be immensely counterproductive in the long run, since it leads to low morale, lack of trust and an underlying sense of animosity, which do nothing to contribute to a productive, satisfying work environment.

With regard to competitiveness, the main thing to consider and constantly assess is the degree to which our approach and that of our employer's is positively proportioned. There is no way that a sense of healthy, constructive competitiveness is going to disappear (and, as we've seen, this would not altogether be a desirable development), but we need to be vigilant that it doesn't spill over into becoming a negative dynamic.

Most important of all, never forget to take a moment to congratulate yourself if you've achieved a significant goal (this doesn't have to be an earth-shattering achievement, just especially important to you). By taking a short time to enjoy the sense of satisfaction that comes with success, we're using a basic stress-diffusing technique. In contrast, always moving on to the next task without feeling any sense of pleasure, accomplishment or closure is in the end, going to contribute to making us feel we are on a permanently pressured professional treadmill. This is one of the surest ways of eventually getting burnt out by an unhealthy accumulation of negative stress.

'Macho' Working Hours

We live in a culture where so many of the signals we receive suggest that in order to be successful we have to be tough, capable of demonstrating endless supplies of mental, emotional and physical stamina and totally committed to the task in hand. This is the case even if it means that we, or our families, have to suffer in the process. It's no accident that these signals are most commonly to be found in many working environments. The desire for maximum profit, increased competition and the drive to get the largest possible market share often results in staff at various levels of the workplace being required to put in an ever-longer working day. There are particular fields that have had this 'macho' reputation for quite some time; examples include medicine, education, military training and involvement in a high-profile law practice.

However, especially since the 1980s, this desire to see how staff perform when they're exhausted and under immense pressure has also spilt over into the business world. Working ever-longer hours each weekday, taking work home in the evenings and losing weekends to professional requirements are now often regarded as being part of the package. And as I heard one dynamic, extremely successful medical consultant say at a conference, the basic message is 'If you can't stand the heat, get out of the kitchen'.

This may all be well and good, especially for those who have constitutions that thrive on living on the 'edge', where their drug of choice is the adrenaline surge that comes from immense mental, emotional and physical pressure and being constantly challenged. For many others the reality is quite different, since we now have an acknowledged problem with those who push themselves in any working environment too far for too long. This problem is called professional 'burn-out', and especially involves those who were high-fliers at an early stage in their profession and who were seduced into thinking that they can deal with any amount of negative stress for any length of time.

The mistaken assumption is that the body has infinite resources for bouncing back from long hours spent at a demanding job, too little sleep and a generous consumption of alcohol, cigarettes and coffee in an effort to maintain the pace. Although it is true that we can keep going for an often impressive amount of time by relying on the impetus of pressure, unless we're blessed with an exceptionally cast-iron constitution we will eventually discover that we have reached our limit. Once this happens the symptoms of burn-out are almost certainly going to follow. These include difficulty in achieving a refreshing night's sleep, lack of emotional and mental resilience that may take the form of mood swings, irritability and extreme fatigue. Another symptom is a tendency not to recover well from minor illness and in fact, with each episode of illness we may feel worse in relation to the one before.

The secret in managing punishing working schedules is to ensure that we have enough compensation in the form of practical stress management techniques, and that we are able to enjoy regular breaks within which to revive our energies. By making these a priority that we never let slip, it should be possible to rise to the occasion of challenging professional schedules without paying the unacceptably high price of burn-out. Always bear in mind that if you recognize the early signs of burn-out on the horizon, it is high time to take stock and some action to diffuse the symptoms of negative stress.

Bullying Tactics

It is a sad fact that the tendency to bully raises its head in early childhood, making the lives of many schoolchildren an acknowledged misery. It would be good to think that this is purely and simply down to a lack of maturity, and that, once we move into adulthood bullying would become a thing of the past.

The worrying truth is that bullying can thrive in the workplace in the guise of bosses who use bullying techniques to intimidate staff, or colleagues who may use subtle or not so subtle bullying tactics to feel superior and more influential. The largest UK-based study of workplace bullying (entitled *Destructive Conflict*) revealed that a staggering one in ten employees consider that they have been bullied at work during a six-month period. One in every seven victims of bullying behaviour claimed they were affected on a daily or weekly basis by abusive behaviour.

The core issue with regard to understanding the reality of bullying is one of power. In other words, without having some advantage over their victim, bullies can't work effectively. This power can take the form of being physically stronger, mentally brighter, materially richer, physically more attractive or occupying a position of seniority. Bullying can also take the form of subtle or not so subtle techniques that serve to make us feel less confident or powerful, and as a result less able to defend ourselves. This can be especially problematic at work, since serious bullying can cause us immense psychological distress and pressure, while also making it more likely that we won't be able to do our job with sufficient confidence and flair to do things well. In severe cases, we may be at risk of suffering from symptoms of anxiety, sleep disturbance or depression, especially if we feel that we are powerless to take positive steps to improve our situation.

In a TUC guide entitled *Keeping Well At Work* it was been suggested that there are specific organizational 'flashpoints' that can create a fertile ground within which bullying in the workplace can thrive. These can include any of the following:

- highly competitive atmospheres
- serious cuts or other radical changes that are about to happen within the company
- generally insecure working conditions (see below for more about this subject)
- 'macho' managerial styles
- little opportunity for communication between levels of staff and senior management
- excessive professional demands being made on staff
- no recognized procedures in place for bullying tactics to be fairly, confidentially and professionally dealt with.

Some professional bullying situations are obvious and self-evident, involving shouting and generally aggressive or overtly sarcastic behaviour. Others, however, involve subtler pressures and forms of undermining behaviour where we feel confused as to the best action to take.

If this seems to be the case, you first of all need to establish that there really is a bullying problem here, rather than an over-reaction or over-sensitivity to another's behaviour. Do what you can to mentally stand back from the most recent situation that has made you feel uncomfortable, and try to evaluate the incident that has occurred in as objective a light as you possibly can. Were the comments or behaviour of the other person justified or genuinely unfair? Could you imagine reacting the same way under similar circumstances? Was the person involved just having a bad day, or do you feel that this sort of behaviour forms a repeating, negative pattern?

If, on objective assessment, you come to the conclusion that you are being bullied, it is important to take sensitive, positive action in order to rectify the situation. If the bully is a colleague and you have a sympathetic, fair boss with whom you can communicate well, the situation should be fairly straightforward to deal with.

Sadly, many workers find that the bullying may be coming from a senior level, or may even be built into the corporate ethos (for instance, targets that are completely unrealistic or working hours that are unreasonably punishing).

If we feel bullied by our boss or line manager, we need to identify someone at work we can trust and take into our confidence. This could be a union representative, friend or human resource manager. Keeping an unfairly stressful situation of this kind to ourselves only makes us feel more tense, and often taking the action of verbalizing our anxieties helps to clarify issues, making an appropriate course of action clearer. Some professional organizations employ harassment advisers, whose job involves giving confidential advice to those who are being bullied about appropriate action that can be taken to solve the situation successfully and fairly.

Keeping a written record or diary can also help give a reliable picture of the situation to others who may need to become involved. Useful information to be noted should include dates, times and brief details of unfair incidents, plus your own feelings and the response given. It may also be helpful to keep any useful notes, memos or e-mails that support your case.

Approaching the bully yourself is generally not the most advisable course of action, because of the unequal nature of the relationship that has already been established. Should you decide to take this course of action always make sure to work out in advance just what points you need to make as clearly and concisely as possible. You must also bear in mind that being assertive is not the same as being angry: in fact, once we've moved from making our points as calmly and clearly as possible to an angry state, we have become disempowered rather than more assertive. It will also be useful to take notes during the meeting, writing down briefly what was discussed and the general outcome. This will be helpful if the result of the face-to-face contact wasn't as positive as hoped for.

In addition, some companies have confidential help lines that you may benefit from, or a counselling service that can be accessed through an employee assistance programme.

The main thing, as we can see from all of the advice given above, is that bullying is a serious problem with serious potential consequences. As a result, the most important thing is to take positive action of some kind, rather than getting progressively stressed out by dwelling on the unresolved problem.

Job Insecurity

Today the concept of 'a job for life' has vanished. The days are long gone when it was a perfectly normal ambition to embark on a profession with a clearly-defined career structure. This allowed for entry at a young age and guaranteed employment until retirement – provided, of course, sufficient promise and commitment was shown at appropriate points along the career path. Although a proportion of careers still allow for long-term progression (such as medicine and law), increasingly large numbers of others concentrate on short-term contracts of employment. Since these are often for a very short period (involving anything from six or twelve months to a couple of years), it tends to create a general sense of insecurity and impermanence within the workplace.

This sense of insecurity can also lead to a pervading atmosphere of needing to show excessive professional zeal and enthusiasm as far as working hours go. For example, it may specify in a contract that our working day requires us to be at work between the hours of 9.00 a.m. and 6.00 p.m. If others are working until 7.00 p.m. or later, we can easily begin to feel that if we leave on time we will look as though we aren't one of the 'team players'. If we're on a temporary contract which is about to come up for renewal, this can bring a huge psychological pressure to bear on us so that we may feel we will look like a slacker if we go home on time.

Resisting these sorts of pressures can be difficult and requires us objectively to decide whether it is more productive and efficient to work all the hours we can, or if making sure we don't get burnt out is going to be the more sensible option in the long run. If we decide on balance that we do need to put in more hours at work for a while to accomplish a specific task, we also need to take some care of ourselves outside of work. This should help to ensure that the temporary pressure doesn't trigger some of the stress-related problems outlined in the previous chapter.

If we work in an atmosphere where there's an almost palpable, pervading sense of job insecurity, we need to take positive steps to create our own oasis of calm that we can tap into when we need it. These will be covered in detail in Chapters Four and Five.

Low Morale
Low morale is often the result of a potent combination of the sort of bullying tactics, hyper-competitiveness, macho working hours and job insecurity discussed above. If all of these continue unhindered, it's almost inevitable that any workforce will suffer by becoming discouraged, edgy, short-fused and pessimistic. The good news is

that in the same way that a depressed atmosphere is contagious, the opposite is also true.

When we feel calm, in control and positive, it has an effect on those around us, who may also begin to realize that any situation can potentially be seen from a 'glass half empty' (empty being negative) as opposed to a 'glass half full' (full being positive) perspective. When faced with a difficult challenge, those of us who take a 'glass half full' approach will be looking for possible solutions, and as a result, once these become apparent, we will be ready to take appropriate positive action in order to solve the problem.

A 'glass half empty' mind-set, however, will not support us in reaching any positive conclusions, since we're likely to feel swamped by the problems. There is also a bigger problem that tends to spring from a pessimistic approach, which is called catastrophizing. When we feel negative and depleted of morale, we are also at greater risk of feeling a rising tide of anxiety about the problems facing us. Once this happens and we're at the mercy of an anxious mind-set, the next step is often to start to visualize the potential catalogue of disastrous outcomes that may be ahead. When anxiety really gets going, it can be amazing to realize how fertile an imagination we can have for creating detailed images of disaster.

The saddest thing of all is that this sort of activity does nothing to help us solve the problem at hand (which is usually of minute proportions in comparison to the catalogue of catastrophe which our imagination will have created). Instead, the experience of catastrophizing makes us feel drained of energy, full of trepidation and generally disempowered. The last three are powerful obstacles to the art of problem solving, and as a result will leave us with the feeling that our situation is hopeless.

In order to resist a general atmosphere of dismal morale we need to start with ourselves, ensuring that we feel sufficiently mentally and emotionally balanced and resilient to keep a realistic perspective ourselves. In order to give ourselves the best chance of doing this successfully, we need to retreat from unrealistically negative feedback for long enough to clear our own perspective.

We need to use relaxation techniques to rest and replenish the mind and emotions, use creative alternative medical support to keep us positive when the going gets tough, avoid falling into nutritional traps that can unwittingly contribute to mood swings, and make sure we don't get deprived of regular, good-quality, sound sleep. In other words, we need to take on board most of the advice given in the rest of this book if we're going to have the best chance of remaining positive and mentally and emotionally resilient. This is of paramount importance as many of us can't change our working environments, but can change our lifestyles to give us a fighting chance of remaining positive.

Personal Stressors at Work

This section looks at the inability to delegate and concentrates on some of the recurring negative patterns that may be sabotaging our 'inner poise', satisfaction, creativity and productivity at work without our even consciously realizing it. We may be subject to these limiting behavioural tactics ourselves, or we may be on the receiving end of these patterns at the hands of our colleagues. Either way, we need to identify these issues as problems before we can do anything positive to improve our professional situation.

Lack of Delegating Know-how
This is a particularly draining and devastating problem in the busy workplace, since it almost certainly guarantees that work will not be accomplished efficiently and promptly. In addition, those of us who just can't bring ourselves to delegate effectively are almost certainly going to suffer from unreasonably high and steadily escalating negative stress levels. These, in turn, leave us open to becoming likely candidates for emotional, mental and physical burn-out. In order to delegate effectively we need to acknowledge that there is a problem in the first place, since those who find it difficult to relinquish even the tiniest amount of control will often respond by adopting a pose of denial when the question of delegating arises. For simple, positive strategies that encourage effective delegating skills, see Chapter Three.

Inability to Set Effective Boundaries
This can become an insidious problem on several levels within the workplace. Some of us may suffer at the hands of managers who may have fallen into the trap of being too familiar and relaxed at

one minute, only to become distant and domineering when crisis hits. This creates one of the most stressful working environments, since it leads to a general sense of uncertainty and insecurity at work. This is due to the way in which nothing is quite so stressful as unpredictability. However, those managers and colleagues who are effective at establishing consistent boundaries are doing a significant amount to make the professional environment an effective and productive one.

Those who are self-employed also face a different problem with regard to effective boundary-setting. These issues tend to revolve mainly around working and non-working hours. The eternal temptation that must be resisted when we're self-employed is the tendency to work all hours available at any given time. This may be necessary at specific times of high pressure, but it is only advisable for short periods of time. This is because trying to do without identifiable leisure time doesn't make us more productive, but has quite the opposite effect of making us work more slowly and in a less focused, efficient way.

An additional concern with regard to setting effective boundaries at work is connected to arranging our workspace in such a way that we work as easily and effectively as possible. This requires organizing our workspace so that we can access information as quickly as possible. This usually means keeping papers and other urgent material filed away in an accessible system, whilst also making sure that vital information stored on computer is also organized in a way that it can be identified and retrieved as effortlessly as possible. Not being able to locate urgently needed material under pressure can be responsible for a great deal of unnecessary negative stress and waste of nervous energy at work.

We'll explore how to set the most effective boundaries in all of these areas in Chapter Three.

Poor Organizational Skills
If organizational skills don't come easily, they can be learnt through using some simple techniques that will be outlined in the next chapter. These are basically an amalgamation of the skills employed in boundary-setting, prioritizing tasks, learning effective delegating skills and managing work surroundings and colleagues more effectively.

Before we tackle improving organization skills, we need to establish that this is a problem area in the first place. We can do so by answering the following questions:

- Are you always struggling to meet important deadlines?
- Do you find it difficult to identify the tasks that need urgent attention?
- Are you easily distracted from the task in hand?
- Do you feel constantly or easily overwhelmed by work?
- Do you find your surroundings make you feel unmotivated, uninspired and/or discouraged because of their untidy nature?

If you answered 'yes' to most of these questions, then it's pretty certain that developing some simple organizational skills will go a considerable way towards reducing your background negative stress levels. What must be borne in mind from the outset is that the best place to start exploring and developing these skills is at the most basic level. Above all else, always resist the tendency to be radical and over-ambitious, since this is almost certainly going to lead to procrastination and stalling before taking the necessary action.

As a result, the common problem that emerges from this scenario is that we don't manage to get going at all. However, by starting with the simplest, most practical steps we are far more likely to get on with making a start, and success is more surely going to have a chance to follow. For practical advice on how to start developing simple and effective organizational skills, see Chapters Three and Four.

Low Self-esteem
This can be one of the greatest stress factors of all, since it leaves us open to bullying and other forms of manipulative, damaging behaviour at work and elsewhere. Feeling negative and insecure about ourselves can also give rise to a more insidious, subtle form of damaging behaviour where we may begin to subvert ourselves through lack of confidence or lowered self-esteem. This is one of the most essential forms of subversion to resist, since it can stop us from even attempting tasks that allow us to be noticed. If this happens, our chances of promotion are going to be severely compromised.

If short-lived feelings of damaged self-worth emerge after a distressing life event such as a painful relationship break-up or family tensions, it may be possible to get back on course again by confiding in a close friend or having a course of alternative or complementary therapy. We may consider taking up a new activity that broadens our horizons and gives us a confidence boost, or taking time out to treat ourselves to things that make us feel good about ourselves again. This could involve going on a special holiday, having a 'make-over', or just making sure we have plenty of time to rest and revive ourselves both physically and emotionally. It helps to bear in mind that each of us is different in this regard, and that what suits one may be totally inappropriate or ineffective for another.

Those of us who fall into a different category may have felt a gnawing sense of failing confidence for a long time and are likely to benefit from taking a different approach to the problem.

In this sort of situation, seeing a trained counsellor may be very helpful in allowing us to safely and constructively explore what has led us to this problematic, self-limiting way of thinking. Alternatively, if we feel very strongly that we are carrying around emotional, repeating patterns that we find hard to resist or break free from, cognitive behavioural therapy may be well worth considering.

This therapeutic approach concentrates of helping us to identify any negative thought patterns that have been laid down in childhood. Once we've determined that these exist and how they manifest themselves for us, we're in a position to change the situation. It can be immensely liberating to discover that we have a choice as to how we respond to any given situation, however challenging it may seem to be.

Of course, opting for professional advice and treatment doesn't rule out the possibility of drawing on some of the strategies mentioned above as well. This is especially true of exploring treatment with complementary therapies, since complete medical systems such as homoeopathy can have an important supportive, positive role to play as we explore psychological insights, emotional conflicts and other possible areas of trauma.

Environmental Stress at Work

While a great deal of de-stressing work needs to be done from within, by learning how mentally and emotionally to switch on the relaxation response, it helps to remember that external factors can also play their part in reinforcing undesirable feelings of negative stress and pressure. These may include any of the factors listed below.

Sick Building Syndrome

These days many large offices are air-conditioned and centrally heated. While in principle this leads to a convenient, readily-controllable system for maintaining a desirable temperature through all four seasonal variations, the practical results are not always so successful or desirable.

Many problems stem from the way in which air-conditioning often requires the treated building to be hermetically sealed. As a result, if the system isn't working at peak efficiency, or if it breaks down, it may not be possible to open windows easily. Air-conditioned buildings can also create a very dry atmosphere that can aggravate problems with allergies and sinus congestion. Too powerful central heating systems can also aggravate both of these problems, while hermetically-sealed buildings (when double-glazing is added into the equation) can also contribute to the spread of minor infections such as colds, sore throats and coughs.

In order to combat some of these environmental problems at work, make a point of trying to get out into the fresh air at lunch time for a brisk walk. Even if you are in a city-centre location (with all its attendant problems in the form of atmospheric toxins), try to find the nearest green space and enjoy a stroll for as long as you are able to.

At work it is also worth making use of simple, effective breathing techniques whenever you feel the pressure starting to build up. These are described in Chapter Five.

Poor Lighting

Inadequate natural and/or artificial lighting can be responsible for a whole host of subtle problems that affect our health and ability to focus and concentrate. Common problems can include tension headaches, eye strain, feeling emotionally flat or low, and difficulty in mentally focusing for any extended period. Widespread use of fluorescent lighting, so often found in offices and supermarkets, is one of the greatest burdens inflicted on those of us who suffer from migraines that can be triggered by irregularly flickering lights.

Lack of natural light during a long winter can also be significantly responsible for some of the low moods that descend at mid-winter, which linger and refuse to lift until a sunny spring is well established. This condition has been named seasonal affective disorder (SAD for short), and can be rectified to an impressive extent by using full-spectrum lighting. This can be used at work in the form of a light box that is designed to sit on a desk, or at home in the form of custom-made light fittings that mimic the positive effect of being exposed to sunlight.

Open-plan Office Pressures

Lack of privacy when taking an important phone call, the intrusion of unwanted conversations, incessant ringing of other people's phones, and the generally raised noise levels that are part and parcel of open-plan office arrangements will do very little to make us feel relaxed. As there is not a great deal we can do to change the layout of the space in which we work (unless we happen to be the boss), it makes sense to do as much as we can to make the work space that we use as stress-reducing as possible. For practical advice on how to set about doing this, see Chapter Four.

Toxic Emissions from Office Machinery

Modern workplaces can also bring added problems to the ones already listed above. These include toxic by-products that come in the shape of emissions from office equipment. Indispensable as these high-tech accessories to modern office working have become, there is a significant price to be paid in the form of toxins that can permeate our workspace without our being consciously aware of it.

Undesirable effects from daily exposure to the toning fluid used for photocopying machines, and odourless ozone gas generated by computers and fax machines that get trapped inside offices due to lack of effective ventilation, can trigger or aggravate symptoms without our making the link. One of the common problems that can be aggravated by contact with computer-generated ozone gas includes irritation of the mucous membranes of the eyes and the nasal passages. As a result, working in a modern open-plan office where there are banks of computers arranged side by side can make low-grade allergy symptoms and sinus congestion worse.

If we add to this equation the adverse effects that appear to arise from exposure to toxic molecules found in glues and solvents that are routinely used to attach carpet to its backing, modern offices can clearly be a low-grade health hazard. However, all is not lost as there are simple and effective ways we can look after ourselves at work, especially when stress factors are high. These make up the fabric of Chapters Four and Five.

ChapterThree

Breaking the Deadlock

Now that we have identified where the main flashpoints lie with regard to negative stress in the modern workplace, it is time to start exploring the solutions. Each reader is likely to have found that certain areas discussed in the previous chapters have a particular resonance for them, issues that cause problems or noticeably limit their productivity or creativity. Once these issues have been isolated it is much easier to take action in order to improve the situation.

For those who recognize that their problems are linked to focus and organizational issues at work, this chapter will be the place to start. Readers who feel that these are less pressing concerns than the problems with their immediate environment may choose to head straight for Chapter Four, returning to this chapter later to get a broader overview of additional practical strategies that are invaluable ways of keeping stress in balance.

Positive Strategies: Putting Basic Boundaries in Place

The key to effective stress management in any area involves avoiding the temptation of looking at the global problem. This is likely to lead to feelings of being overwhelmed by the sheer scale of what needs to be done, rather than giving us the impetus and inspiration we need to tackle poorly-managed stress levels. If we choose instead to break down the tasks that need to be dealt with into manageable chunks, we can envisage ourselves dealing with one at a time, and before we know it, we will have made significant inroads into tasks that may have been worrying us for a considerable time.

It may sound too obvious for words, but before any stress reduction plan can be put into operation we must first make a conscious commitment to making it work. Feeling half-hearted will only result in lacklustre solutions at best, and no progress at all at worst. However, embarking on a stress-reduction plan with enthusiasm and clear intent will enable us to reap rewards in the long run that may surprise us by the sheer extent of the improvements. Not only should we find that we focus more effectively on whatever task is at hand, but we should also find that those niggling, low-grade physical symptoms that seemed here to stay (such as difficulty in sleeping, general fatigue, indigestion and/or tension headaches) disappear as if by magic. This process may be so subtle that we don't even notice how much better we're generally feeling until someone else draws our attention to it or we suddenly realize that we haven't needed to buy a packet of painkillers for a while.

It helps at the outset to remember that making these proactive, positive changes shouldn't feel like a solemn chore, otherwise we will almost certainly give up at the first hurdle. Instead, see your starting point for action as the first exciting step in setting a positive energy cycle in motion.

The momentum for this sort of liberating transformation tends to go something like this: once the decision to take action has been made, we already feel better about doing something constructive about problems we may have been putting 'on hold' for some time. Even taking small steps to change this situation will make us feel better about ourselves, so we're likely to generate more positive responses at work. This will reinforce the boost to our self-esteem, making it more likely that we will have the enthusiasm to carry on. This gives us the motivation to look at other areas of our lives that we may have been feeling less than happy about. These lifestyle issues could include wanting to cut back on alcohol, coffee, sugar, junk food or cigarette consumption. Once this shows signs of getting under control, we're almost certainly going to feel much more healthily in command of our lives, plus we are also going to sleep more deeply and refreshingly as a result of the positive dietary modifications that we're making. For a more detailed explanation of why this should be the case, see Chapter Six, which shows us how the quality of what we eat and drink can have a profound effect on making us feel chilled-out and relaxed or strung-out and tense.

As the positive cycle we've set in motion gets more established and stronger, we will also discover that we have more sustained, resilient mental, emotional and physical energy and vitality. We may find that we want to make time for exploring systems of fitness that help balance mind, body and emotions even more effectively, while also encouraging us to wind down and relax. Excellent choices include yoga, Pilates or t'ai chi. In this way we reinforce the positive cycle is re-enforced, giving us the best chance possible of rolling with whatever punches life may throw at us whenever the pressure at work builds up. Supported in this way, we may not be able to take negative stress out of life, but we will be giving ourselves the maximum opportunity for dealing with it as effectively and productively as possible. Always remember that unmanaged negative stress has a draining effect on all aspects of our lives, including our mental performance, emotional balance, intimate relationships, sense of well-being and general experience of health and vitality. As a result, managing negative stress effectively benefits all of these areas of our lives and more.

At all costs fight the impulse to subvert yourself and your efforts. Many of the best intentions come unstuck as a result of lack of self-belief, and an often unconscious attachment to what is familiar. When this happens, a change of even the smallest kind can seem threatening, and before we know it we begin talking ourselves out of acting to improve our situation. Should this happen, resist it at all costs and just focus on making the first small steps towards taking control and initiating action. Once the process has begun, it will get progressively easier to fight any instincts towards self-sabotage.

Don't be discouraged if you fall off the stress management wagon occasionally. It's only human to make mistakes from time to time and it can sometimes be positively healthy, since it stops us acting like saints! It is also inevitable when we're trying to learn new ways of dealing with negative stress that there will be times when the temptation to fall into more familiar habits will just seem too tempting. When this happens, it is very important not to beat yourself up metaphorically, but to accept that it has happened, learn something useful from the experience and get back on track again as soon as possible. Most important of all, never let one glitch discourage you from continuing to explore further positive changes.

The Pivotal First Steps

The simple steps described below form the bedrock of the most essential organizational skills. They may seem terribly obvious, but they will enable us to focus on getting moving so that we can deal with issues which we may have got into the habit of avoiding for a very long time.

Prioritizing

We can't get anywhere if we don't have a very clear idea of where to start, so developing effective prioritizing skills is of paramount importance if we want to make the most of additional stress-management skills at work, such as delegating.

We will never be able to see issues clearly in order of importance if we rely on constantly turning them over in our minds. Rather than clarifying what we're thinking about, this practice tends to have the opposite effect of making us more confused and uncertain about the issues we're considering.

Instead, always make a point of writing down points to be considered, since list-making can have a very therapeutic role in enabling us to look at stressful issues more objectively. First of all, once you've made a list of tasks that need consideration, you may be surprised to see that they aren't as overwhelming as they may have felt when you were mulling them over in your head.

List-making of this kind can be immensely helpful in a number of different and equally valuable ways. They can be designed to help us consider the pros and cons of two opposing ways of looking at an urgent or difficult situation. When used in this way, lists can provide us with an important decision-making tool. Alternatively, jotting down a series of points can enable us to consider how urgently one issue demands attention in comparison to another. If it's difficult to reach a decision straight away about which issue should take priority over another, having made the list, put it to one side for an hour or so, and get on with something else in the meantime. One you've given the mind a break, you may find that you see things more clearly when you consider them freshly again. If there's time, sleeping on an important issue can also be helpful, since the subconscious will have had a chance to work things through while you sleep. This is why we can often go to bed thinking about a problem with the solution presented to us when we wake up.

We can also use simple techniques to visibly separate those issues that need more urgent attention than others that are still important but not critical. One of the best and most straightforward is a graded underlining system. All that is required is to give those points that must be acted on most promptly three underlinings, others that come next in the pecking order two, and those that can wait (but not be forgotten about!) one underline.

As each task is done, make sure you cross it off the list. Strange as it may sound, there is something extraordinarily therapeutic and satisfying about seeing accomplished tasks being crossed off a list. This appears to be connected to the way in which making an achievement (however small) concrete and visible creates a sense of accomplishment and satisfaction.

Often we will be perfectly able to identify tasks that need prioritizing by ourselves. However, with regard to more complicated issues where a great deal is at stake, or for concerns that we feel too closely involved in to handle objectively, consulting someone whose opinion we value and trust can be immensely helpful. This will especially be the case if the person we consult has a gift for cutting through any unnecessary information that may be clouding our own prioritizing judgement.

Delegating

Learning the skill of effective delegation is one of the most liberating experiences we can enjoy, especially if we have previously felt stressed to the hilt because of the feeling that we've had too many tasks crowding in on us. But it is important to stress at the outset that delegation isn't the same as 'passing the buck' or just wanting to duck out of or evade pressing tasks. These only lead to avoidance, which is the opposite of a proactive positive stance.

When we delegate appropriately, effectively and sensitively, we are positively empowering ourselves and others. The skill is to have the confidence to know when to let go of tasks that can be done as well or even more effectively by others. In order to benefit from these skills we need to be able to relinquish control when it's appropriate: something that many of us may find much more difficult than it initially sounds. However, the benefits that come from learning these skills are so great that they more than repay making the effort. But it should be stressed that firm boundaries must be put down in order for effective delegating to take place. For instance, the person who is being delegated to must be in no doubt about the full responsibility of what is being required of them. If this isn't made crystal clear, then a stressful situation is almost certainly going to be the result.

Before we start the process of identifying tasks that can be appropriately delegated, we need to apply the principles of prioritizing outlined above. Once we've done this with any series of pressing tasks, we'll be much better placed to see how many jobs are genuinely urgent and which ones can be done later.

In addition, considering a list that is organized in this way allows us to evaluate how many of these jobs need to be done by us personally. If the list is more manageable than we initially thought when turning the issues over in our minds, we may be pleasantly surprised to discover that these jobs are in fact quite achievable by ourselves.

However, if we discover that there are a number of tasks that are very pressing and we can't possibly get around to dealing with all of them in the desired period, we have to consider delegating a proportion of these. To make this work to its maximum positive effect, it will be necessary to select colleagues who we are confident will do the job in question promptly, efficiently and to our own work standard.

If we feel a general sense of resistance to even the basic idea that we need to part company with some tasks it is time to consider whether we are holding on to inappropriate amounts of work due to a desire to keep control. This is especially the case if this happens under circumstances where it's obvious that, even with the best will in the world, we can't possibly get everything done by ourselves in time. What follows from this essential dynamic is that we may feel subconsciously afraid that if we relinquish a certain amount of power (however appropriately) we might come to be seen as dispensable. This underlying insecurity can, without our consciously realizing it, be responsible for a great deal of stress in the workplace because it can encourage us to hold on to a volume of work that we can't possibly deal with, which in the long run has the negative effect of making us feel swamped and disempowered. In contrast, learning the skills of confidently letting go can lead to our beginning to feel more productive, efficient and powerful in the workplace.

Most important of all, when delegating is done appropriately and with the required amount of consideration and effective communication, we're likely to feel the sheer pleasure and exhilaration that comes from not feeling indispensable. In reality, in any professional situation none of us is truly indispensable, since however much we may be missed if we leave a position, the work will continue to go on with or without us. Once we appreciate that this is the case, we will be free to enjoy professional challenges and demands without feeling as though we're carrying the responsibility of the world on our shoulders. The interesting irony is that once we adopt a less burdened and fraught approach to work issues, we are likely to be pleasantly surprised at how much more focused and productive we can be at work. In reality this isn't too surprising, since all that's happened is that we've adopted a pivotal stress-reduction technique that frees us from the draining and distracting effect of unmanaged negative stress.

One of the best ways of encouraging an original, empowered response to a problem is to suggest that the person who has brought the problem to light might think about possible solutions themselves. With any luck, having given the issue due consideration, they will come up with one or more possible ways of dealing with the issue.

Should the situation occur again with the same member of staff, the question should be asked once more. Very quickly that member of staff is likely to start coming up with suggested solutions rather than problems, and eventually as their confidence grows they should begin to take the initiative to solve problems by themselves.

Communicating

In order to delegate efficiently we need to have effective communication skills so that we can explain exactly what is needed and how it needs to be done. Above all, communication skills should be used in such as way that what we say is clear and unambiguous, but not patronizing.

Apart from the benefits that effective communication skills bring within the sphere of delegation, the ability to communicate well brings much broader benefits when used in the workplace. Always remember that effective communication works both ways: those in senior positions will benefit by getting to know how their staff are responding to fresh initiatives, and those further down the hierarchy will benefit greatly from seeing effective communication skills in action by senior management. When managers do this well, it allows their staff to understand how and why certain decisions may need to be made that affect them directly. When this doesn't happen, there is always the potential for misunderstandings and resentment to develop, which can have a very undermining effect in the workplace.

Whatever side of the communication equation we happen to be on, the following suggestions can help facilitate the process of effective understanding:

- Always focus beforehand on the essential points that need to be communicated. Before making anything clear to anyone else, it is important that we first have it clear in our own minds.

- If necessary, make a few brief notes in order to prompt yourself, but always avoid the temptation to make these too lengthy or detailed because they will only prove to be a source of confusion rather than the clarity you're striving for. A few key words of each point should be all that's needed to serve the purpose well.

- Consider how the other party is likely to respond to what you have to say, while also being prepared for reactions that may surprise you. By taking the time and effort to anticipate the reactions we might meet to any suggestions we have to make, it's possible to move things along more smoothly and successfully.

- Some of the best communicators are the best listeners. It helps to remember that listening needn't be a passive skill, but can be an active one when we really listen to (rather than mechanically just hear) what the other party is saying. Not only does this save a great deal of time (labouring for a while under misunderstandings only wastes valuable time, since the situation has to be clarified before we can move forward effectively), but being listened to well almost always makes the other person feel more positive and appreciative.

- When listening to someone, it helps if we try to avoid some of the most common negative habits that we may have developed without even consciously realizing it. Never look at your watch when someone else is mid-sentence: you may simply see this as a practical way of assessing how much time you have left for discussion, but to the person who is speaking it's going to seem downright dismissive. Other gestures that can have a negative effect on positive communication include avoiding eye contact when an important point is being made, yawning, glancing out

46

of the window, or any other signal that suggests that you are being distracted. You may be all ears while you're doing this, but this is not the message that other party is going to pick up.

- One of the basic rules of effective communication involves remembering that anger and aggression are not the same as assertiveness. If we want to convey an especially important point and the situation is a little tricky because the other party is feeling less than agreeable to what we have to say, it is more essential than ever to make sure that we remain assertive. This in turn involves our being as calm and clear as possible about the issues involved. Once we've shown our frustration we have lost power rather than gained it: when we are furious it is very difficult indeed to hold on to what we need to say in a focused way. In this situation it is highly likely that we're going to be far more easily diverted into an emotive discussion about issues that may not be especially relevant. Adopting an assertive stance is quite different, since it allows us to stick to the points that we need to communicate in the clearest, focused way. It also helps any heated discussion from building into an unnecessarily acrimonious exchange. Once this happens, communication has temporarily broken down and it may take some time and a great deal of hard work to get it back on track.

- When involved in any discussion or presentation, always try to consider how you would choose to be spoken to; otherwise, without our realizing it, we may slide into adopting a tone that may seem patronizing or insensitive. By thinking along these lines we are far less likely to lose sight of the other person's point of view – something which can be an enormous help in making us more effective communicators.

- Be aware of the other person's body language in order to try to gauge how they may be responding to what you have to say. Sensitive and accurate interpretation of another's body language can give us a clue to how someone is responding well before we have any verbal confirmation. Obvious clues include folding the arms (which can indicate feeling vulnerable or defensive), furrowing the brow (feeling concerned or perplexed), or becoming obviously physically restless (which may convey a feeling of uneasiness about the issue, or just indicate that things have gone on for too long).

Compromising

It is important to reject the idea that all compromises have to involve weakening our position: on the contrary, seeing the potential for a working compromise can sometimes empower both parties to solve a difficult problem. Intelligent and considered compromising is especially important in a situation where being too rigid and absolute may have nothing but negative consequences in the long run.

The ideal compromise occurs where all parties involved indicate that they're willing to yield a little ground in exchange for a working solution that benefits the other parties who are willing to negotiate in a similar way. Compromise that involves one party obviously giving up more than others tends to be less successful, since this can lead to resentment and a general sense that decisions may have been made in a less than fair way.

Of course, for compromises to be made most effectively we ideally need first to draw on the communication skills outlined above if we're to get the most out of any discussion about reaching an effective halfway house.

In addition to working as harmoniously as possible with others in order to find a working compromise, we also need to find mechanisms for cutting ourselves some slack at appropriate times. This is likely to be especially appropriate for those of us who may have little trouble in helping our colleagues to establish effective compromise solutions to problems, but may be very unyielding with regard to ourselves. This is particularly true if we tend towards perfectionism at work and at home, with the result that we may constantly push ourselves too hard in the search for an elusive ideal of perfection. Without realizing it, if we feel that accepting anything less than the ideal solution is a form of failure, we will be continually setting ourselves up for a sense of dissatisfaction, disappointment and disillusionment as we simply can't achieve perfection all of the time.

Finding a working compromise for ourselves within this sort of context often involves bringing into play effective skills of prioritizing and delegating, which should also empower us to be able to ask for help when it's appropriate.

Before we reach an effective compromise to a problem we need to be able to have a realistic, rather than an idealistic, view of what is possible. Once we are very clear in our minds what can realistically be achieved, we are on much firmer ground as we explore possible ways of dealing with the situation. When this basic skill is learnt, it can be an invaluable tool in helping us to enrich our personal lives as well as our working experience. On the other hand, constantly adopting a non-negotiable stance is likely to significantly increase our negative stress levels at work and at home.

Chapter Four

The Healthy Workplace

The previous chapter considered ways of getting ourselves mentally focused on practical methods of dealing with some of the most common triggers of negative stress reactions. Now it's time to consider some simple, effective strategies that we can apply to not only getting our external environment in order, but also to creating a workspace that makes us feel motivated and inspired. Although this is written primarily with the workplace in mind, it helps to remember that this advice can be equally helpful when applied at home, especially if we are self-employed.

De-stressing our Immediate Environment

It is astonishing to consider how powerful an impact our surroundings can have on the way we feel, often without our consciously being aware of it. Messy, disorganized environments don't just slow down the pace at which we work, but can also reinforce feelings of stress without our even registering the negative effect it's having on us. Time taken to rectify the situation and start transforming our workspace into somewhere that makes us feel motivated and focused is time extremely well spent. If we're feeling bogged down and unable to cope properly as soon as we settle down to work, it means that it is time to take a look around and evaluate just how our work area looks and feels.

Above all, fight the temptation that suggests this is a luxury you can't afford. Regard it as an investment that is likely to yield significant benefits further down the line. Also bear in mind that whenever we meet with strong resistance to an idea (sometimes to the point of outright denial that there could ever be a problem in the first place), this often suggests that this an area of sensitivity. As a result, it's probably something that would benefit from some attention.

Clutter-clearing

In many ways, the degree to which we're surrounded by disorganized documents, folders, unopened or unacted upon e-mails, letters and memos can reflect our state of mind. it's highly likely that if, when we are working, we can constantly see material that reminds us of tasks we've been putting off for too long, it's only going to reinforce any lurking sense of negative stress that we may have been trying to ignore.

Practically speaking, not being able to access information from documents quickly and easily when we need it is inevitably going to make work much harder and more frustrating to do in the long run. This applies as much to documents kept on computer as it does to hard copies that may be buried in an inaccessible heap.

On a more esoteric level, from the perspective of feng shui it is suggested that hoarding heaps of unnecessary papers, books and magazines (especially at floor level) prevents positive, productive energy from flowing. Whatever we may make of this or not, it's undoubtedly the case that attempting to work your way around heaps of clutter is the opposite to inspiring, and will inevitably hold things back rather than encourage them to move forward smoothly and speedily.

Heaps of clutter also bring another practical problem in their wake in the form of dust-gathering, which can aggravate allergic rhinitis, especially when dust-traps are combined with central heating and/or air-conditioning.

If by now you have decided that a spot of clutter-clearing is definitely in order, the following simple advice should help to get you started:

- Take a hard, objective look at whatever is in the heaps and take out any items that demand urgent attention. Anything else that's pending but not absolutely pressing can be put in a 'to do' tray. Those items that are extremely old and no longer relevant can be shredded or thrown away, but remember to retrieve any items that have important information in them that is useful for future reference: these should be rescued and filed away.
- You are likely to need to do the same with your computer (since those of us who have problems keeping documents in order and dealt with promptly often find the same pattern repeats itself

with any material held on computer). Follow the same pattern as outlined above, putting important stray documents into folders and deleting anything that is no longer relevant. One of the most effective ways of keeping base-line levels of stress at work low is to make sure that we always back up computer files. This may sometimes be a nuisance but, as I know from my own experience, it can ensure that we are not driven to desperation by losing essential information.

- Above all, avoid the temptation to hoard anything that is obviously no longer relevant in the mistaken belief that it 'just may come in handy' at some point in the future. This approach is one of the clutter-clearer's greatest enemies and must be resisted at all times. When evaluating the importance of any item, try to be as clear, objective and rational as possible about its genuine value. Sometimes it helps in making this decision if we take this simple rule on board. When in doubt ask yourself: how long ago was this item used? If the answer is a year or more, then the chances are that you can happily dispense with it.

- Consider ways of rearranging your workspace to create a sense of having more space, light and air. Simple ways of doing this may involve fitting in more cupboard space to allow for important items to be stored away and, if the budget allows, swapping older models of high-tech gadgets for more streamlined, smaller versions.

Improving Lighting

Inadequate or problematic lighting can cause a number of subtle problems without our even realizing it. An increased susceptibility to tension headaches, neck strain, eye problems and lack of concentration are just a few of the distracting symptoms that can arise from consistently poor lighting at work. Shoulder tension can also be a troublesome complication that stems from inadequate lighting (especially when we work at a desk all day). Should this set in as an ongoing habit, we're certainly unlikely to be able to ignore the problem due to persistent or severe aches and pains in the neck, shoulders, upper and lower back.

Tell-tale clues that suggest we should be considering improved lighting include any of the following:

- a tendency to squint or wrinkle up the eyes and forehead when reading any documents or concentrating on a VDU screen
- finding that mistakes are being routinely or frequently made as a result of mis-reading work.
- an awareness that the workspace feels gloomy and likely to induce a feeling of lack of alertness or drowsiness.
- a troublesome consciousness of flickering fluorescent lighting (this is especially negative for those of us who suffer from migraines, since irregular or flickering lights of this kind can actually trigger an acute episode)
- frustration with inflexible lighting over our desk – 'inflexible' meaning that it cannot be moved and therefore cannot be angled to light any documents that are especially difficult to read, on account of this fine print or layout.
- Apart from these mechanical aspects of poor lighting, there are also more subtle problems that can arise from inadequate natural lighting that can have a significant effect on raising our stress levels at work. This will especially be the case for anyone who knows that they are candidates for seasonal affective disorder (SAD). As we've already seen earlier in this book, common problems associated with this condition include feeling low, depressed and demotivated during the winter months due to lack of sunlight. If, in addition, we work in gloomy, badly-lit spaces, it's easy to see how this may aggravate already existing problems associated with SAD.

If you feel that you may have a problem with less than positive lighting arrangements at work, the following practical steps are worth considering.

- If SAD appears to be an issue (and a holiday in the sun during the darkest winter months really isn't a practical option), it is well worth considering investing in a full-spectrum light box for your desk. Designed to create the effect of natural sunlight, this may help discourage the 'blues' from descending as ruthlessly and regularly during the tough winter months. Those who have a more flexible budget may decide to have full-spectrum light fittings installed at home as well (or escape for a few weeks in the Caribbean instead!).
- If you regularly read from documents placed at the side of your

computer screen, always make sure that you have a desk light that can be easily moved and angled to illuminate the document effectively.

- When working at home, it's worth replacing outdated fluorescent lighting with more modern alternatives that are easier on the eyes. This is especially is important if you suffer from regular headaches.
- Consider the amount of natural light that comes into your room. If there's more than enough (due to working next to a large window, for instance), this may be perfectly adequate and is likely to benefit you by increasing the possibility of remaining focused, decisive and generally on the ball. However, if this is very much not the case and you are aware that your workspaces don't allow for any contact with natural light, it is time to take action in order to compensate. Those of us who work at home can rectify the situation by placing uplighters and other free-standing lamps strategically around the room. When we don't have this freedom, it may be necessary to have a word with the boss if he or she is approachable, sympathetic and has good communication skills. Otherwise it may be helpful to raise the issue with an occupational health adviser if poor lighting is genuinely causing problems at work.
- Consider whether a different choice of colour or texture for curtains or blinds may have a lightening effect on your workspace. We may not be able to change the amount of sunshine that is available each day, but we do have a choice about how much light we allow to filter through our windows.
- Don't forget to engage in a spot of clutter-clearing. This may be especially helpful if a messy workspace is having a negative effect on the amount of natural light that's able to filter into your work area. After all, being surrounded by towering heaps of documents or other unnecessary items really won't help in achieving a general sense of exhilarating openness, space and light.

Dealing with Postural Problems

When we are tense, many of us respond by adopting familiar postural habits that often occur as an unconscious reflex. This process is sometimes referred to as body armouring, a term that conveys quite effectively what happens to our bodies. Since this often involves tightening the muscles in the face, neck, shoulders, arms, hands and upper back, we are left with these muscles feeling tense and braced. The instinct that leads us to do this is essentially a protective one, but it's sadly misplaced as it has the effect of making us feel considerably more stressed in the long run. This is even more the case if we adopt these postural reactions on a frequent or permanent basis, as a number of stress-related problems are thought to result from negative postural habits of the kind listed above. Some of these include tooth grinding, jaw joint problems (often referred to as TMJ problems), recurrent tension headaches, shoulder tension, and upper and lower back pain. TMJ problems usually result in misalignment of the temperomandibular joint (the hinge joint that links the upper and lower jaw bone). The main symptom that can stem from TMJ problems is a tendency to recurrent migraines or headaches. Since this is a relatively newly-discovered condition, it is often best diagnosed by a dentist who can offer treatment in the form of a dental splint that can be worn overnight.

If we consider that these are basic negative postural habits that can come into play whenever we feel threatened or stressed, we don't need to have over-active imaginations to appreciate how vulnerable we are to these problems being magnified at work. For many of us, work is a honey-trap for tension and stress for all of the reasons discussed in the previous chapters. Since negative postural habits can be aggravated by poor seating, badly-aligned workstations or repetitive actions needing to be performed over a lengthy period, we need to deal with these if we are to avoid becoming more mentally, emotionally or physically stressed at work than we need to be. Simple ways of guarding against negative postural habits may include any of the practical measures detailed below.

- It is very difficult indeed to adopt and maintain optimum postural alignment if we are sitting in an uncomfortable chair for most of our working hours. Chairs that don't allow for adequate, comfortable support of the back, or those that are the wrong height and don't allow our feet to rest easily on the floor can aggravate ongoing postural problems. Those of us who are mainly involved in desk-bound work should make it a priority to check that chairs and workstations are arranged in such as way that we feel comfortable when we work. Tell-tale signs that

suggest it may be time to seek advice about suitability of equipment could include any of the following niggling problems:
- – neck or shoulder pain
- – tension or recurrent pain anywhere in the back
- – aching in the hands, wrists or fingers
- – recurrent headaches.

Items to check out include:
- – the suitability of using a neck rest
- – how comfortably our knees and legs fit under the desk in any position
- – the need for a wrist rest when doing a lot of keyboard work
- – the need for a foot rest.

If we're in doubt about any of these, an opinion from an occupational health expert should help. Alternatively, if we are self-employed and suffer from any of the problems listed above, we may be able to get helpful, practical advice from an osteopath, chiropractor or Alexander technique teacher.

- If we have ongoing or severe postural problems that are causing us discomfort, rather than relying on painkillers as a 'quick fix' solution, it is time to think about more satisfactory ways of dealing with the underlying problem. If we've been especially tense recently and know that we are compensating by clenching any available muscle (tell-tale areas include the face, jaw, shoulders, hands and thighs), we should consider seeing a massage therapist who will be able to work at encouraging areas of tension to relax. This effect is likely to be enhanced if the therapist is also trained as an aromatherapist. Alternatively, for more deep-seated problems that affect joints as well as muscles (especially if we know these are centred around the neck, shoulders and back), we would do well to consult a chiropractor or osteopath.
- If we spend a lot of time speaking on the telephone and don't wear a headset, it's very beneficial to avoid the temptation of trying to hold the receiver between a raised shoulder and the ear on that side. This is often done in order to leave the hand free on that side to take notes, but this habit can trigger or exaggerate severe

problems with neck tension and shoulder pain. If your job involves regular telephone conversations (especially if these tend to be stressful in nature more often that not), it is certainly worth requesting a head set in order to avoid developing negative postural habits.

- Many of us know we're very unfit because we spend most of the day sitting at a desk, in our cars and slumped in front of the television to relax. If this is the case, it's high time to think about taking up a form of exercise that will benefit our state of mind as well as our posture and overall state of physical fitness. Always bear in mind that exercise doesn't have to be a structured affair, but should be an activity that we feel is enjoyable and fun. Depending on our personal temperament, this could involve any of the following: team sports, swimming, badminton, salsa or line dancing, or anything else that appeals to us and gets our bodies moving. Before starting any activity it is advisable to have a basic health check from your GP, especially if you are a newcomer to exercise. Ideal forms of movement that concentrate on optimal postural alignment and which also include a de-stressing component include yoga, t'ai chi and the Alexander technique. Although the latter isn't a system of exercise, it can be an invaluable therapy in revealing to us how we may be responding to stress by tightening up areas of our bodies. Learning how to react differently and more positively as a result of this therapy can help us deal with postural problems while also freeing up a significant amount of energy. This is due to the way in which constantly holding our muscles in a clenched position without our conscious knowledge can use up significant amounts of energy.

Combatting Environmental Toxins

When we work in conditions where we are surrounded by computers, photocopiers and faxes our bodies may have to deal with a steady, low-grade toxic bombardment from the chemicals involved in some of this high-tech equipment. VDU screens also bring problems in the form of generating fields of static electricity.

If we work in a modern office and are concerned about some of these problems, we should take a proactive stance to try to counteract these negative factors in our working environment. These can include any of the following;

- If possible sit three feet away from your VDU screen and try to take a break from sitting in front of the screen for a few minutes every hour.
- Green plants are generally thought to have a beneficial effect on our environment at work and at home. This is due to the way they appear to play a beneficial role in helping to positively balance the amount of oxygen in the atmosphere through their own process of respiration. If we are concerned about being on the receiving end of low-grade radiation as a result of regularly sitting in front of a computer, we should consider investing in a special radiation control screen. In addition, we may choose to buy a variety of cactus that is claimed to have a beneficial effect when placed next to a computer. Garden centres have these labelled accordingly.
- Ionizers are also thought to be a helpful aid in balancing negative and positive ions in the atmosphere. When we experience a surge in negative ions it is rather similar to the after-effect of a thunderstorm, when the atmosphere feels clear, calming and invigorating. However, when positive ions are dominant it has the opposite effect; we tend to feel muzzy-headed and lack concentration and focus. By installing an electric ionizer we will be helping to create and maintain the optimum balance between positive and negative ions in the atmosphere. As we can imagine, this may be of particular benefit if we tend to feel sleepy, headachy and lacking in concentration at work.

QuickTips on Instant Unwinding

Here are some quick tips for rapid relaxation when we feel the pressure building up at work. While these are very helpful as fast-track strategies for instant relaxation, do bear in mind that they are only short-term strategies. For maximum benefits in effectively reducing and managing stress levels we need to employ the more long-term solutions outlined in the next few chapters. However, the quick tips detailed below are an excellent way of starting the process.

Relaxing Facial Muscles
Without our realizing it, we can hold an enormous amount of strain and tension in our faces. Next time you feel under pressure, watch

what is happening in the area around your jaw: the chances are that, without you being consciously aware, your jaw is clenched shut and lips pursed together. In order to loosen up these muscles in double-quick time, bring your attention to your jaw joint and consciously relax this area. You should find that if you do this correctly, your bottom jaw moves slightly downwards and as a result your lips relax and part ever so slightly.

Shoulder Circles

Too many of us tend to react to stressful stimuli by tightening up the large muscles that run down either side of our neck and holding our shoulders in a tight position lifted up towards our ears. Not only is this extremely uncomfortable, but it also makes it highly likely that we may suffer from tension headaches and upper back pain. Tight shoulders can also be aggravated by any job that requires us to sit or stand in a set position for any extended length of time. This can quickly be remedied by doing a few shoulder circles whenever this area begins to feel uncomfortable and unpleasantly tight. Raise your right shoulder in a slow circular motion, moving in a backward direction for a total of five circles. Then reverse the process, circling forwards for five. Repeat the process on the other side. You may find that one cycle that works on both shoulders is enough, but you can continue the process as long as you feel it needs to release any accumulated tension.

Shoulder Shrugs

These can also break a cycle of tension in the shoulders whenever we feel the pressure building up. Before beginning, try to let both shoulders relax and drop downward slightly. Then raise both shoulders together as you breathe in, moving them as comfortably close to your ears as possible. Hold them here for a few seconds, clenching the muscles of your upper arms at the same time, before letting both shoulders relax downwards as you breathe out. You should find that this returning position gets a little lower with each shrug as the shoulders become increasingly relaxed. However, always make sure to make this a gentle movement, taking care never to push the process to any point where it causes pain or discomfort. Always listen to what your body is telling you: if anything you force it to do causes pain, that is the most effective signal your body has to let you know that something is wrong.

Alternate Nostril Breathing
Provided we can do this discreetly, this yoga-based breathing technique is one of the fastest, most effective tools we can use to clear our heads and feel instantly calmer. Curl the middle three fingers on your right hand into your palm, leaving your thumb and little finger extended. Place your right thumb gently against your right nostril so that it effectively closes it. Now breathe in slowly through your left nostril for a count of four, before closing both nostrils by placing your fourth finger gently against your left nostril. Keep both nostrils closed for a count of four, before releasing your right nostril and breathing out for the same count. Repeat the same process, beginning with the right nostril; once this is complete, you've done one cycle. This may be enough to achieve the desired calming effect, but you can continue for longer if you feel it will be more helpful.

Relaxing the Eyes
Many of us may find that we build up a lot of tension in the muscles around the eyes when we concentrate on work for any extended period. This is likely to be especially true for those of us who tend to stare at documents or a VDU screen without realizing that we haven't blinked for a while. One of the best ways of relaxing and giving the eyes some extra sparkle involves a technique called 'palming'. Extremely quick and simple to do, all it involves is cupping the palms of both hands and placing them gently over closed eyes. Make sure the pressure of the hands is firm, but gentle and comfortable. Leave the hands in place for a minute or so as you gently breathe in and out. If you have the time, you may choose to do a visualization exercise as you relax during a palming session. For practical advice on how to do this, see Chapter Five.

Inhaling Calm
When the tension is building at a fast and furious rate, combat negative stress and take control by inhaling a drop or two of lavender essential oil from a tissue making sure the tissue is an inch or two away from the nose. This should immediately help you focus on the task in hand in a calm and clear way.

Using Oils for Energizing and Relaxing

It is not difficult to understand why aromatherapy is such a popular choice for so many people. The use of essential oils in the form of massage, inhalation or diluted in a fragrant bath is one of the most accessible and pleasurable ways of enjoying the benefits of any complementary therapy.

The benefits that come from using essential oils are very flexible in nature, since their use can be adapted to whatever need is paramount at any given time. When we need to be stimulated and refreshed, we have a choice of revitalizing oils at our disposal, while there are others that can be equally effective at supporting us in winding down and relaxing.

The appeal of aromatherapy is also linked to its very 'hands on' nature, with little fuss or paraphernalia being involved in its use. We can also draw on our own instincts when choosing oils, since whichever choice we make needs to be appealing to us.

Practicality is also high on the list of advantages when we become familiar with the possibilities of using aromatherapy to ease the pressures and strains at work. The most straightforward and discreet method of benefiting from the therapeutic properties of essential oils is undoubtedly inhalation.

This can be enjoyed most subtly by decanting one or two drops of a selected essential oil onto a tissue or handkerchief and gently sniffing. If we want to be more high-tech about it and provided colleagues don't mind sharing in the benefits of vaporized essential oils, we may choose to use a custom-made electric vaporizer. For the more decadent, silk wrist rests that are impregnated with essential oils which have a soothing, anti-inflammatory quality can be obtained.

These are some basic rules that are helpful to keep in mind if we're exploring the use of essential oils for the first time:

- Always bear in mind that essential oils are astonishingly concentrated, and that very little is needed to achieve the desired effect. As a basic guide, no more than four or five drops need to be used in a vaporizer, while a drop or two would be more than enough when inhaling directly from a tissue.
- When applying essential oils to the skin in the form of a massage

blend, always make sure that the oils are diluted in a carrier oil first. As a rough guide, no more than one drop of oil should be used for every teaspoon of carrier oil. Any of the following make suitable carrier oils: sweet almond, avocado, jojoba, walnut or wheatgerm.

- Adding oils to a warm bath at the end of a busy day at work should also be a sparing business. Five or six drops maximum will be enough to make the bath water deliciously fragrant. Always remember that oils should be dripped gently on the surface of the bathwater after the bath has been run, otherwise there is a strong risk that the beneficial, aromatic effect of the oils will have been compromised by evaporation.
- In order to give your essential oils the best chance of their maximum shelf life, always make sure that the cap or stopper of each bottle is kept firmly in place. This is very important because once a bottle has been opened, its chances of degeneration increase. This is due to the potential for the oil to come into contact with oxygen in the air. This process is called oxidation and can damage the purity of concentrated oils.
- Light can also have a damaging effect on essential oils, so bottles should be kept in a cool, dark place well away from the direct rays of bright sunlight.
- Safety first: always store essential oils at home out of the reach of children. Although on the Continent essential oils are sometimes ingested under the strict direction of medically-trained practitioners, this is a practice that is not done in the United Kingdom.
- In order to avoid any damage, make sure that essential oils don't come into contact with any synthetic materials, such as rubber. This is important because, due to their highly concentrated nature, some oils can cause these materials to perish. Highly polished or varnished surfaces can also be damaged by accidental spills of essential oils.

Energizing, Refreshing Oils
Any of the following are excellent for giving us an energy boost and clearing the head whenever we feel we are finding it hard to maintain the pace:

- black pepper
- rosemary
- coriander
- peppermint
- lemon
- grapefruit.

Mood-balancing Oils
- If we're feeling 'burned out and blue', the following essential oils have a reputation for being natural antidepressants:
- bergamot
- geranium
- lemongrass
- rose otto
- ylang ylang
- clary sage.

Relaxing, De-stressing Oils
Relaxing and de-stressing oils include:
- juniper berry
- cedarwood
- roman Camomile
- frankincense
- ylang ylang.

Chapter Five

The Relaxation Response

We may not be able to decrease the amount of negative stress and pressure that comes at us at work, but we can learn how to react to it in the most positive way. This involves knowing how to activate the relaxation response when we need it as discussed in Chapter One. Once we've become skilled and practised at doing this, we are likely to find that we can cope much more effectively with stressful crises.

We will also have the comfort of knowing that we can retreat to this safe psychological haven whenever we need some breathing space within which to work out how to deal with whatever crisis has arisen. There are also important spin-off effects that come from enjoying regular periods of relaxation and meditation. These come in the welcome form of enhanced concentration, improved decision-making ability, better sleep quality, fewer mood swings and enhanced mental, emotional and physical energy levels.

It has also been suggested that regular practice of relaxation exercises, meditation or relaxing breathing techniques may have an important role to play in helping combat a range of stress-related symptoms. These may include anything from high blood pressure to tension headaches and irritable bowel syndrome. We've already explored some of the reasons for this positive effect in Chapter One, where we look at the relationship between the autonomic nervous system and the development of stress-related problems.

However, it is important to understand at the outset that what we're considering here isn't a 'quick fix', but an integral part of a healthy lifestyle. Once regular relaxation becomes a routine part of each day it brings long-term benefits with it. The chances are that we're also going to look forward to this part of each day as a chunk of time that is so pleasurable that we are unlikely to want to give it up once we've become used to it.

When we become quite familiar with what is involved, some of the techniques that follow can all be applied at work quite discreetly without anyone being aware of what we're doing. Of course, if we want to engage in a longer session in more peaceful surroundings, we can also choose to do a daily relaxation session at home.

Strategies for Using Breathing Techniques at Times of Stress

Controlled breathing is beneficial in stressful situations. It is not difficult to do and it takes only a little time to practise the methods described below.

Diaphragmatic Breathing

The process of respiration is a curious thing. We all know that we can't survive if we stop breathing, but so many of us just take it for granted and pay little or no attention to it, leaving it to take care of itself. This is mainly because the process of respiration is regarded as an involuntary bodily activity: in other words, we don't consciously have to control it in order for it to keep on happening.

While this is basically true (after all, if we had to deliberately initiate every in and out breath it would get tedious in the extreme!), we do have the capacity to ensure that we breathe in such a way that benefits body and mind. This sort of calming and energy-balancing breathing technique is called diaphragmatic breathing. It is an invaluable technique to learn and should form the bedrock of any stress management teaching.

This is because breathing in a rapid and shallow way, only bringing the muscles of our upper chest into play, is something that we all unconsciously tend to do when we're feeling stressed out for any reason. This is part of the body armouring reaction discussed in the previous chapter, which sadly has a counterproductive effect on our bodies and minds, making it highly likely that we're going to feel more tense and stressed with each breath. This is due to the way that breathing rapidly and shallowly has an adverse effect on the ratio of oxygen to carbon dioxide in our systems. As a result of this continuing imbalance, common symptoms tend to arise such as breathlessness, palpitations and a general sense of pervading and escalating anxiety. As we can readily imagine, none of these feelings is going to make us calm or clear-headed when we find ourselves in a particularly stressful position at work.

The good news is that we can effectively reverse this negative process by learning how to breathe slowly and smoothly, utilizing as much of our lung capacity as possible. Once we know how to do this effectively, we will be able to draw on this skill whenever we feel the pressure heating up. At first it is best to learn how to master this technique lying down or sitting in a straight-backed chair, leaving ourselves plenty of time to get accustomed to how it feels. However, once we have become really adept at doing breathing for relaxation, we will be able to call on its support in situations where no one needs to be aware that we are doing anything different at all.

First Steps

It helps to be prepared if you're a newcomer to relaxation, making sure that you have taken steps to ensure that you are going to feel as comfortable as possible during a session. Bear in mind that clothes need to be loose and cosy (body temperature drops by a significant amount during deep relaxation) and that your surroundings need to be comfortably warm but not stuffy. If there is too little ventilation and the room becomes over-muggy, there is a good chance that you may be tempted to fall asleep. Pleasant as this may be, this really doesn't achieve the same beneficial effect as deep relaxation.

- Choose a room that is as tranquil as possible and free of any annoying distractions. If necessary, unplug the telephone to prevent stressful or unwelcome interruptions.
- If you feel comfortable lying on the floor, use an exercise mat or thick towel to lie on, making sure you choose a spot that is well away from any cold draughts.
- If you prefer to sit upright during relaxation should choose a straight-backed chair that gives comfortable support to the whole of the spine. Make sure that you feet rest comfortably and securely on the ground.
- When lying down, let the arms rest gently on the floor a little distance away from the body, with the backs of the hands making gentle contact with the floor. The palms of the hands should face up towards the ceiling, and the fingers should naturally and gently curl slightly inwards towards the palms. Once the legs are relaxed, they should naturally fall apart so that their position echoes that of the arms. If this doesn't feel comfortable for the lower back, bend the knees towards the body, ensuring that both feet make

comfortable contact with the floor. Also make sure that the lower back doesn't arch (this will put strain on it) but also makes comfortable gentle contact with the surface you are lying on.

- Once you feel quite comfortable, place one hand lightly on the belly at roughly the position of your navel and close your eyes (this will help you focus and concentrate better). Breathe quite normally for a few breaths before consciously breathing out as fully as you can.

- As you take in a gentle, large breath, consciously fill your lungs as much as possible from the top to the bottom. If you fully achieve this, the hand resting on your belly should rise slightly. Don't worry if you can't achieve this effect at first, and on no account force the breath. In order to benefit fully from relaxing breathing techniques of this kind you need to work in harmony with what your body is able to do. In time you should find that possibilities increase comfortably and quite naturally, rather than causing any sense of pressure or discomfort. Always remember what you are aiming for is progression rather than perfection.

- Once you have taken a full breath, pause for a second before releasing the breath as you exhale fully. As you so this you should find that the hand resting on your belly returns to its original position as the belly deflates ever so slightly.

- Continue breathing in this way for as long as it feels comfortable. If you are in a sitting position, the same rules apply, since you should be aiming to feel your lungs filling fully with air on the in breath and emptying themselves as completely as possible on the out breath. The hand resting around the area of your navel is there just as a guide in order to confirm that you really are using your full lung capacity. As you get increasingly familiar with what is involved, you won't need this extra help in order to measure how well you're doing.

- Above all, never force the pace of the breath, since this is more likely to cause stress than release it. What you are aiming for is a gentle, rhythmical movement that is no more erratic or forced than the ebbing and flowing movement of a wave against the seashore.

- If at any stage you feel light-headed or dizzy, don't panic. Just resume normal breathing for several breaths and you should feel the light-headedness lift.

- After taking enough calming breaths to feel relaxed and replenished, you might want to end the session or go on to one of the guided relaxation or meditation exercises described below. If you do decide to stop, always make a point of never sitting or standing up abruptly, since this can cause a general sense of disorientation and dizziness. This is especially to be avoided by anyone suffering from low blood pressure, who is likely to feel extremely faint on getting up too quickly from a reclining position. Instead, take care to open your eyes and bring your conscious attention back to the room. Have a good stretch and slowly turn on to one side. From here you should find it very easy to slowly raise yourself into a sitting position. When you feel ready, move into a kneeling position before gently progressing to a standing pose.

Ujjayi Breathing

Once we have mastered diaphragmatic breathing techniques for calming the mind and body, we can use this invaluable tool whenever we feel we want to slow down the pace. This could be appropriate if we are maddeningly late for work, in a confrontational or difficult meeting, or if we have just been landed with an extra demanding task at work that is going to challenge us considerably.

However, there are also going to be times of stress at work when we feel that what we need is access to more mental and physical energy to help us out of a tight spot. For this purpose it will be helpful to learn another technique used in ashtanga yoga called Ujjayi breathing or 'fire breathing'.

- Begin by sitting in comfortable, peaceful surroundings that allow you the space to concentrate on what you are doing without interruption.
- Take a conscious full breath in, at the same time attempting to concentrate on gently tightening the muscles around your throat. Make sure that you do not overdo this, since there should be no sense of uncomfortable, over-constriction in the throat. If this is being done correctly, you should be aware of a soft, hissing sound on the in breath.
- Gently exhale, still keeping the muscles around the throat slightly

taut. This sound should be a slightly different tone to the in breath (think back to *Star Wars* and the sort of sound Darth Vader made breathing behind his mask).

- If this feels comfortable you can take six Ujjayi breaths before having a rest and fully relaxing the area around the neck and throat. Once you become familiar with what is required, you can repeat this cycle of six breaths whenever you are in need of a quick boost of mental and physical energy (provided, of course, you don't sound too much like Darth Vader).

Guided Imaging Techniques

Once we have become familiar with what is involved in diaphragmatic breathing, if we have the time we can choose to take a further step into deep relaxation by doing a guided imaging technique that creates the effect of having a mental holiday. At the end of a harassing day this can be a marvellous way to just switch off and unwind.

- Use the same routine that has been suggested above in the diaphragmatic breathing section to get yourself calm and fully relaxed. Keep your eyes closed and take slow gentle breaths, still making sure never to force the depth or the pace of their rhythm.
- When you are ready to begin, call to mind the image of a place that you may find extremely beautiful, uplifting, relaxing or inspiring. This could be somewhere that you have actually visited; this tends to be the best choice to make since you will be calling on quite detailed memories of the place during this exercise. It could be an idealized place that may have made a huge impression on you from a photograph or on television. If you have an especially fertile, visual imagination you may prefer to dream up a place of your own making; it really is up to you and what is going to make you feel most relaxed, inspired and comfortable. It really does not matter whether you choose an indoor or outdoor scene, or whether it happens to be an invigorating seashore, tranquil woodland or vibrant country setting: it just needs to be an environment with which you feel you have a special connection or rapport.

- As you mentally explore your chosen scene, become aware of all of the sights, sounds and sensual impressions that are an integral part of it. You may choose to lie down and experience the sense of profound tranquillity that floods your body in this special place, or you may feel that you want to continue to walk and explore more of the scene you have entered. As you discover more and more aspects of your surroundings, feel as though you are being drawn deeper and deeper into a state of peace and relaxation.

- As you breathe in, imagine that your body is being filled with a warm golden liquid that symbolizes a deep sense of well-being, peace and calm. As you breathe out, visualize any tension, worries or stresses that may have been nagging away at you leaving your nostrils in a cloud of vapour. If it makes this any easier, you can choose a colour for this vapour.

- Before you leave your guided imaging technique, you may choose to imagine that you have a protective aura around you that can be any colour you prefer. At a later stage you may wish to call this protective aura to mind if you feel that negative stresses are beginning to pile up and get to you.

Progressive Muscular Relaxation

Progressive muscular relaxation is a technique that can be combined with diaphragmatic breathing and the visualization technique outlined above. However, it also provides us with a complete relaxation exercise in itself that can be of particular benefit to those of us who feel that we carry tension in particular muscle groups. Common sites for this sort of problem include the face, neck, shoulder and upper back muscles. By concentrating on isolating these areas and consciously tensing and relaxing them in turn, we will be doing a great deal practically to relax and release stiffness and discomfort from these parts of the body.

- Start by adopting the reclining position described above with your eyes closed. Breathe steadily and rhythmically, bringing your attention to the muscles of your head and face. Scrunch the facial muscles and hold for a moment or two before completely letting go; your lips may part slightly as you release the muscles around your jaw. You should find that these muscles feel softer and more relaxed than when you began.

- Lift your shoulders up towards your ears, clenching the shoulder muscles and holding your arms rigid with clenched fists: if you do this correctly, you should find that your arms rise an inch or two above the surface on which you are lying. Let go of the tension, allowing the muscles to soften in the shoulders and all the way down the arms and hands.
- Move your way consistently down your body in this manner, deliberately tightening and relaxing the major muscle groups as you go.
- If as you work your way down the body you encounter any areas of particular tightness and tension, you are likely to need to spend longer on these areas, gently encouraging them to relax and unwind. Other, more relaxed parts are going to demand less attention and can be passed over more quickly.
- When feel fully relaxed all the way down to your feet and toes, it's time to bring your attention back to your surroundings. Gently start to make small circling movements with your feet and flexing movements with your toes. Do the same with your hands, slowly moving the fingers. At this point you're probably going to feel that you want to take a large, long stretch. Finally, open your eyes before slowly bringing yourself to a sitting position as described above.

A Simple Meditation Exercise

Anyone who mediates on a regular basis tends to become extremely enthusiastic about the benefits from daily practice. As well as helping to reduce the tendency to develop a wide range of common stress-related conditions such as anxiety, insomnia, high blood pressure and muscle aches and pains, regular meditation sessions have also been credited with stimulating improved levels of concentration. This makes us generally more mentally sharp, creative and productive.

As a result, the sense of focus and purpose that emerges often brings further benefits in its wake, since extra energy isn't being squandered in endless, low-grade worry and anxiety. Bearing this in mind, we could sensibly argue that regular meditation practice brings yet more benefits in its wake, through encouraging conservation of energy that can be put to more productive use than being frittered away on unrealistic anxieties about something that may never happen.

For those of us who are put off by anything that seems rather mystical and New Age, it's good to know that we don't need to take any esoteric beliefs on board in order to reap the benefits of meditation. The process of meditation may be seen as nothing more mysterious than an effective way of switching off the distracting 'chatter' that can go on in our minds, especially when we happen to be preoccupied or under pressure. When we become familiar with practical benefits that come from switching of this distracting dialogue, we are likely to notice that we are far less likely to feel undermined by the draining effect of anxious thoughts. This comes as a very welcome bonus to those of us who spend time involved in jobs that are particularly demanding or stressful.

However ambitious and impressive this may sound, it's very important to bear in mind that the basic techniques used in meditation can seem disarmingly simple. The challenge tends to lie not in the technique itself, but in finding the discipline that is required to get into the routine of regular practice. Ironically, those who would most benefit from the mental relaxation and replenishment that come from regular sessions of meditation often find that they are reluctant to give up to the time to do so. This is a hurdle of perception that is well worth getting over, since the benefits more than outweigh any short-term disadvantages that appear to come from making the time available each day.

How we choose to set about meditation is pretty much up to individual taste. Some of us may find we instinctively focus more easily on an object, such as a candle flame or flower. Others may find that they prefer to generate a mental image from their imagination, while yet more may prefer to use a simple counting technique as the focus of their attention.

- In order to begin, adopt the lying-down or sitting positions described in the above sections.
- If lying down, take a few regular, deep breaths with your eyes closed and visualize an image that appeals to you. Ideally this should be a simple object such as a flower or a candle, since anything more complicated is likely to be a trigger for distraction

rather than an aid to focusing the mind.

- When meditating in a sitting position, sitting cross-legged can become rather uncomfortable (unless your knee joints are very sturdy), so it may feel more comfortable to sit in a straight-backed chair that gives good support to the spine.

- If choosing a sitting position, you may find it helpful to place an object at eye level that you can focus on, rather than relying on an image generated in your mind. This tends to get easier with practice, so beginners are likely to find it more satisfactory to gaze on an actual object in the early days, until the whole process becomes more familiar.

- Mentally focus on your chosen object, putting any other thoughts to one side as they drift into your mind. Don't worry if unwanted thoughts pervade your mind with a vengeance, as this is almost guaranteed to happen when first attempting to meditate. As they present themselves, just calmly avoid paying attention or becoming absorbed in them, bringing the focus of your attention back to the image you are concentrating on.

- As you focus on your chosen object, just observe what is happening to your breathing and gently regulate it so that it follows a steady, gentle rhythm. Ideally it should be possible to synchronize it, so that your inhalation is approximately the same length as the exhalation.

- You may find that it is also helpful to repeat a sound to yourself as you breathe in and out. This should be something very simple, such as any word of a single syllable such as 'one' or any other sound that you feel enhances your meditative state.

- Never rush at the end of a meditation exercise, and always allow enough time to bring your conscious attention back to your surroundings. Otherwise, you may find that by rushing back to activity straight away you feel rather disoriented.

Self-Massage to Release Tight Pressure Points

Massage is one of the very best practical ways of releasing tight or aching muscles. While it tends to be most beneficial to have a treatment at the hands of a trained therapist where we will have the best chance of relaxing completely, for many of us this may be impractical and just too costly on a regular basis. If we are happy to make the commitment to a regular treatment, it helps to bear in mind that an all-over body massage may not be necessary since a weekly neck, shoulder and back treatment may be sufficient. This is going to be of particular benefit to anyone who suffers from regular tension headaches as a result of rock-hard neck and shoulder muscles.

However, if we feel this isn't appropriate, we need not completely miss out on the benefits of massage since we can still encourage a general sense of relaxation by applying some simple self-massage techniques. Getting into the regular habit of working on tight or stiff muscle groups (ideally before a soothing bath) can do an enormous amount to make us aware of areas where we habitually hold tension, as well as feeling extremely pleasurable and relaxing. The latter effect can be enhanced by using a soothing blend of aromatherapy essential oils diluted in a carrier oil. You can experiment by mixing blends dictated by your personal choice, or for convenience you may prefer to use one of the pre-blended formulas available on the market. For advice on aromatherapy oils, see the previous chapter.

Getting Started

Even if you don't opt for a scented oil, always use a good quality carrier oil when massaging the skin. This is very important because it allows the fingers to glide smoothly over the skin without pulling and dragging. This is especially necessary when working on areas of skin that are particularly delicate, such as the neck and around the eyes and mouth. Possible choices of oil include almond, olive or jojoba, or when working on the skin of the face you may decide to use a custom-made facial massage gels.

Relaxing the Face and Neck

Follow these simple steps to give yourself a relaxing face and neck massage.

- Warm a small quantity of oil or gel in the palms of your hands. Begin massaging the neck from the base upwards by moving from one side to the other, using light, upward moving strokes. Try to achieve a steady rhythm where one hand follows the other in a continuous way. Always take care while doing this to avoid any movements that are too heavy, or that pull or stretch the fine skin in this area.

- Move upwards, placing the pads of your thumbs on the skin just below your chin, with the balls of the index fingers resting on the area just above. Work slowly along the jaw in an outward-moving direction, using gentle, small pinching-and-release movements. Carry on doing this until you reach the area just beneath your ear lobes. This sequence can be repeated up to ten times.

- Using the most fluid, firm but gentle movements, take the two first fingers of each hand and starting at either side of the top of the nose, adjacent to the bottom half of the eye socket. Use small pressing movements that work their way slowly and steadily along the cheek bones. Make sure you use the soft pads of the uppermost parts of the fingers and take care to check that your finger nails are short enough in order to avoid their digging into and damaging the delicate skin of this area. Keep going with these small pressure-and-release movements until you reach the TMJ area on either side (this is the jaw joint that connects the lower half of the jaw to the upper). Repeat this movement as often as feels relaxing, up to ten times.

- If the shoulders feel tense, this is an ideal time to pay attention to them. Place the first two fingers of each hand at a central point at the base of the neck, this should be roughly around the area where the collar bones lie. Work steadily outwards with each hand, moving towards the shoulder joint on each side, using the same pressure-and-release movements you should now be getting familiar with. Aim to cover the area in roughly four or five moves. Once you've reached the outer edge on each side, start again at the centre.

Relaxing the Shoulders

Now it is time to move to the back of the shoulders: a well-known magnet for tension in anyone who has a busy, stress-filled life. Start by taking your the three middle fingers of your right hand and use them to massage the large triangular-shaped muscle at the back of the left shoulder. Make sure that the movements are firm enough to release any tension and that they are rhythmical and circular, moving inwards from the outer edge of the left shoulder towards the spine in the centre. Here you spend as long as you feel you need to release any tight, knotted areas of muscle. When you are ready, move on to the other side, repeating the same movements in reverse order.

Releasing the Hands

We hold an extraordinary amount of tension in our hands whenever we are under stress. If you have any doubts about this, just take a moment to observe what happens when you are stuck in a seemingly endless traffic jam on your way to work. The chances are that without any conscious awareness of doing so, you are gripping the steering wheel far too firmly, with the result that your knuckles are likely to look white from the strain of the tightness of the grip. Alternatively, consider the sort of force that you use to grip a pen when writing or hold the handle of a door before you turn it. In all of these cases, most of us instinctively use much more force than is needed to accomplish any of these tasks. The net result is that we are continually squandering unnecessary energy that could be better used elsewhere, as well as holding a lot of tension in the muscles and small joints of our hands.

Because of this unconscious tendency to clench the hands, it makes a great deal of sense to massage them on a regular basis. When we get used to doing this as a regular routine, we're likely to be amazed at how relaxing the overall effect can be.

Start by working up each finger in turn, using the thumb of the other hand on top and the index finger underneath. Massage each digit until you come to the little finger. Repeat this overall treatment three times on each hand before starting to loosen the muscles of the palm. This can be done by using small circular movements that cover the whole area. Repeat this on both sides before working on the backs of each hand using similar small, firm circular movements that move from the base of the fingers to the wrist.

Relaxing the Feet

So many of us tend to ignore our feet unless they start to draw our attention through pain or general discomfort. Since we are so dependent on our feet for a great deal of activity that we take for granted (such as walking freely and easily), it does make sense to pay them regular attention. Massaging the feet can have a surprisingly relaxing effect – something that is often commented on by those who enjoy regular reflexology treatments. But in order to get the maximum benefit from a home massage treatment, we will benefit hugely from first exfoliating the feet in order to remove any rough skin. Once this is done, the skin will accept the soothing, moisturizing effect of the massage oil much more readily.

- Work your way over the whole of the sole of one foot, using firm, circular movements. Spend as long as you need to on each sole, only moving on to the uppers of the feet when the whole area underneath the foot feels as relaxed as possible. You are probably going to have to pay particular attention to the area around the ball of the foot, where a great deal of tenderness can build up. This is especially so if you have a job that involves standing for long periods of time, or if you have a weakness for wearing very high heels. As when working on the backs of each hand, work along the upper part of each foot from the toes towards the ankle, using the fleshy pad of the thumb to exert a comfortable amount of pressure.
- Once both feet are thoroughly relaxed, you may feel that you want to continue a little further up the legs in order to relax the calf muscles and shins. Use long, stroking muscles up the front of each leg with enough oil that your hands glide effortlessly without dragging. Then move to the back of each leg, working from the centre of each ankle using firm, circular movements that eventually cover the whole area of the calf muscles until you reach the area just below the back of the knee joint.

Chapter Six

Nutritional De-stressors

These days it is almost impossible to ignore the important role that food and drinks play in our lives. We are constantly being given more and more information, courtesy of our newspapers, television and glossy magazines, about the latest foods and drinks that are considered to be 'in' or 'out'. The debate about whether carbohydrates (starches such as bread and pasta) are good or bad for us or whether a high fat diet is a nutritional hazard or advantage is almost certainly going to continue for as long as celebrities generate publicity for the latest quick-fix weight-loss plan.

This fascination with what we eat (or don't eat) is further compounded by the popularity of cookery programmes that appear on our television screens with astonishing frequency. It seems as though we've never had so much information about healthy eating, and yet so many of us feel that the science of nutrition continues to be a minefield of confusion and contradictory information.

While its not the job of this chapter to take a detailed look at the whole spectrum of nutrition, the information that emerges will ideally serve to give us a basic working knowledge of some of the fundamental principles of a healthy diet. Clearly the main aim of this chapter is to help us understand how the quality of what we eat and drink can impact in a positive or negative way on our stress levels.

However, by happy coincidence, the less desirable foods and drinks discussed in this section also tend to be the ones that are best avoided if we are striving to change our diets for the better. As a result, this chapter is an excellent place to start if we're thoroughly confused about nutrition and just want some practical, no-nonsense advice to get ourselves moving in a healthier direction. What follows will give us some boundaries to work within, so that we can add in more detailed, sophisticated information as we learn more about the subject.

Nutritional Sabotage: Foods and Drinks to Avoid when Under Pressure

It is ironic that the most common foods and drinks that many of us reach for when we're under pressure and feel wrung-out tend to be the very ones that make us feel more tense, edgy and exhausted in the long run. As a result, we can end up sabotaging ourselves without the slightest knowledge that we're doing so. If this continues for long enough without being corrected, eating and drinking unwisely when we are extremely stressed for an extended period can leave us prime candidates for burn-out.

If we don't have a clue about what these dietary items are, here is a quick run-down of some of the most important foods or drinks we should be thinking of eliminating from our diets, or cutting down drastically when we're under pressure.

Sugar

By now many of must know that too much refined (white) sugar in any form can leave us open to a host of common health problems including obesity, diabetes and increased risk of dental cavities and gum disease. If we gain a significant amount of weight through eating too much sugar, we are also likely to be at increased risk of heart and circulatory problems, especially if we also smoke, eat a lot of saturated fats and don't take any exercise. What we may not realize is that too much sugar in our diets can also make us feel moody, fuzzy-headed or mentally and physically fatigued. This is a combination that is going to be absolutely no help to us at all when we're under pressure and need to perform with a clear head and plenty of stamina.

The problem with refined sugar, which many of us turn to when we need a short-term shot of energy, is that while it does give us a quick-fix energy boost, our bodies respond by bringing blood sugar levels down abruptly. After this initial sugar 'rush' is over, we're likely to feel in need of another sugar 'fix' in order to get us moving. And so the erratic cycle goes on, with increasing amounts of sugar needed to duplicate the initial effect.

Many of us are also likely to be shocked at the sort of foods and drinks that contain a significant amount of 'hidden' sugars. Potato crisps, pizzas, tomato ketchup, baked beans and fizzy soft drinks contain an astonishing amount of added sweetening agents. Obvious sources of refined sugar include chocolate (especially milk or white varieties), biscuits, cakes, ice-creams, preserves and confectionery of any kind.

These are all items that we should avoid when we need to have sustained mental concentration and physical stamina for the reasons given above. However, there is no need to feel bereft since there are excellent, practical substitutes we can enjoy that will give us plenty of energy when we need it most. These are listed in the Nutritional Support section of this chapter.

Caffeine

There is about as much confusion over caffeine as there is over sugar. How many of us mistakenly believe that the best solution to a dip in energy at work is to grab a doughnut or chocolate bar and wash it down with a strong cup of coffee? This is often as a result of skipping lunch because of the need to work through due to lack of time. This is obviously a quick fix, since the combined effect of the caffeine and sugar will undoubtedly give us a short-lived energy boost. However, long-term problem outlined above is sure to kick in if we rely on this strategy for too long.

Caffeine, in the form of a shot of espresso, can of cola or even a strong cup of tea, will raise blood sugar levels and kick our bodies into a state of arousal, so that we seem temporarily to feel sharper and have a surge of energy. Sadly, relying on caffeine to achieve this for us in the long term can give rise to a catalogue of unpleasant symptoms that will undermine rather than enhance our performance, as well as doing absolutely nothing for our sense of emotional equilibrium. These symptoms can include any combination of the following, in any degree of severity:

- palpitations (awareness of rapid or erratic heartbeat)
- irritability
- reduced ability to concentrate
- interrupted or poor-quality sleep
- anxiety
- acid indigestion
- erratic or diminished appetite (this is likely to be exaggerated if a regular shot of caffeine is accompanied by a cigarette).

It has been suggested that anything exceeding two cups of coffee a day is an unwise amount of caffeine to be putting into our systems on a daily basis. However, if we're dependent on eight or nine mugs a day and decide to kick the habit, always remember that it is best to cut down slowly and steadily rather than shock the system by stopping suddenly. The latter is almost certainly going to result in our experiencing symptoms of caffeine withdrawal, which are genuinely unpleasant and can last for as long as a day. If we want to avoid a severe headache and feeling fatigued, jaded and out of sorts, it is far better to cut caffeine consumption by a cup each day, substituting one of the healthier, stress-reducing alternatives listed in the next section of this chapter.

Alcohol

When the pressure is on, having a large drink or two at the end of a nightmare day can seem just the thing to help us unwind and feel good. Sadly, if this becomes a regular habit, the overall effect is likely to be anything but positive. If we're going well beyond our maximum weekly alcohol allowance (14 units for women and 21 for men), we are likely to find that we sleep badly, wake unrefreshed, feel generally foggy-headed and on a mental and emotional short fuse. Since alcohol is an acknowledged mood enhancer, having a drink or two can feel fine when we're having a relaxed and convivial night out. But alcohol has quite the opposite effect on us when we feel tense and uptight or flat and depressed, since these unwelcome feelings are going to be magnified. This is in addition to the other symptoms that are known to be linked to excessive alcohol intake on an extended basis, such as digestive problems (nausea, lack of appetite and stomach pain), increased risk of osteoporosis and severe mood swings.

The trick is to get the balance right so that we can enjoy the odd social drink for the pleasurable thing it is, whilst avoiding the temptation to use alcohol as a regular prop to get us through a demanding day or stressful night. Everybody should strive to have alcohol-free periods where they give the liver a chance to recover, even those of us who are moderate drinkers. Just bear in mind that you're going to sleep much more soundly and feel more energetic and mentally sharper for it. And the chances are that the odd gin and tonic is going to taste much better after having had a rest from it!

Cigarettes

Although obviously not a dietary item, cigarettes often come into the picture when we have a cup of coffee or a drink of alcohol. Having a cigarette can initially be a relaxing experience, but, as with alcohol, the long-term effects are very much less than desirable. Apart from the known health risks that can accompany regular cigarette smoking (increased risk of lung cancer, heart and circulatory disease, bronchitis, osteoporosis, high blood pressure and cosmetic signs of premature ageing), there are more insidious problems that accompany an established nicotine habit. These are linked to the way that, although we feel an initial sense of relaxation when we smoke, the long-term effect seems to aggravate, rather than reduce, the stress response. It also helps to bear in mind that because of nicotine's highly addictive nature, once we go for too long without a cigarette we are almost certainly going to feel irritable, on edge and tense. As a result, if we want to give ourselves the best chance of resilient and optimum health so that we can cope when stress levels are at their peak, we would do well to try to kick the nicotine habit.

If we want to do this, we really need to make sure that we have the maximum amount of practical support we can muster at our disposal. This could include seeking help from an alternative or complementary therapist; acupuncture, hypnotherapy and homoeopathy can be especially helpful. But above all else, the most important motivating factor in giving up smoking is the resolve and determination to really do it. Half-hearted attempts and 'cutting down' seldom tend to yield any lasting positive results, while a bullish determination will give us the best chance of success.

Nutritional Support: Calming, Balancing and Energizing Foods and Drinks

The good news is that, for every item mentioned in the section above, there is plenty we can substitute as a healthy, stress-reducing alternative. This needn't be done overnight otherwise we're probably going to feel pretty groggy for a few days, but we will benefit greatly from cutting down steadily on the items listed in the section above, while steadily substituting those that follow.

Wholegrain, Complex Carbohydrates

It has been established that the foods that give us the best chance of sustained mental and physical energy come in the form of unrefined carbohydrates, such as wholegrain bread, pasta, grains, fruit and vegetables. As a result, if we want a sustaining meal that isn't going to leave us hollow within a short time and eager for more, it's best to go for:

- wholegrain cereals with a piece of fruit
- wholegrain pasta with a vegetable sauce
- wholewheat toast with a small portion of protein in the form of fish pate, poached egg or naturally low-fat cheese.

These should form some of the basic ingredients of our regular diet if we want to have sustained, rather than roller-coasting, energy release.

Unroasted Nuts and Seeds

Nuts and seeds are excellent sources of healthy essential fatty acids that help protect optimal hormonal balance when we're under pressure, as well as being very handy to have at work when we need a quick, tasty snack. If we feel in need of a quick energy boost, a handful of unroasted brazil nuts, sunflower seeds and hazelnuts can be combined with a small amount of dried fruit, such as organic apricots. Although these contain quite a concentrated amount of fruit sugar, its release is buffered by the fibre in the fruit. As a result, it creates an overall less abrupt effect with regard to energy release than the products made from refined sugar mentioned above.

Fresh Fruit

Always have some fresh fruit at work readily to hand (and easy to eat!) whenever a snack is needed. Bananas, apples, pears, plums, apricots, peaches, strawberries and cherries are full of fibre and essential nutrients, while also giving us the energy-boosting effect of fruit sugars. In addition, bananas give us a tryptophan boost. This amino acid is a precursor to the feel-good chemical serotonin, which acts as a powerful antidepressant. It can be found naturally in foods such as bananas, which act as a mild mood balancer when we're under pressure.

Avocados, Dairy Foods, Lettuce and Oranges
These are regarded as having natural sedative properties that can be very helpful to us at times of high stress and pressure, since they can encourage us to unwind and relax if we're feeling tense and irritable. This is largely due to their bromine content, which appears to have a relaxing effect on the body.

Freshly-squeezed Fruit and Vegetables Juices
Juicing fruit and vegetables that are bright red, yellow, orange or dark green in colour will give us a significant helping of antioxidant nutrients. These are especially important at times of high pressure, as they have been shown to help support efficient immune system functioning when stress levels are high.

Herb Oil Teas
Herbal teas can provide us with a delicious range of hot drinks that we can introduce to take the place of caffeinated varieties. The best known of the calming herb teas is camomile, but other blends are also available that contain soothing, stress-busting lemon balm and valerian. Alternatively, if we feel that our stomachs need settling after a major night out, fennel and ginger tea may do the trick. If we prefer sharper flavours to the mellowness of some of the herbal blends, we can explore some of the citrus-based fruit teas on the market. The trick is to experiment until we discover the blends that appeal to us most: after all, it's highly unlikely that we're going to feel relaxed if we have to hold our noses in order to sip a herbal tea that we can't stand the taste of!

Green Teas and Grain-based Coffee Substitutes
If we want a refreshing hot drink with a lower caffeine yield that also contains an impressive array of health-promoting ingredients (such as antioxidants), we could do no better than enjoy the odd cup of green tea. On the other hand, if sometimes we feel we'd like a hot drink that we can add a dash of milk or cream to, we may prefer to try one of the instant coffee substitutes available. These are naturally caffeine-free and are most often made from roasted grains to which natural flavourings have been added. In my own experience, for these to be most successful it tends to be best to forget about the flavour of coffee and to treat these as a different type of drink altogether.

Generous Quantities of Mineral or Filtered Tap Water
Without knowing it, many of us are mildly dehydrated most of the time. If we don't make a point of drinking five or six large glasses of water each day, we are likely to experience problems that are related to low-grade dehydration. This can be slightly confusing, since they often resemble stress-related symptoms. These can include headaches, constipation, skin problems and a tendency to recurrent minor infections such as cystitis.

Basic Benefits of Making Time to Eat: Creating Patterns of Eating that Help Keep Us Energized, Relaxed and Focused

Not only does *what* we eat and drink matter, but *how* we choose to do it also has a significant effect on our mental and emotional balance as well as on our sense of physical well-being. As a result, if we want to enjoy optimum health at work and at play, it does make sense to put some thought into not just eating well, but also making sure that we adopt healthy eating patterns. These include any of the following:

- It is an ironic fact that our natural inclinations tend to sabotage us when time is tight and we are required to meet pressing deadliness. Faced with this situation, many of us may be tempted to skip lunch and grab a sandwich or bag of crisps at our desk (if we're lucky!). While this won't cause major problems as a one-off fire-fighting strategy, it is certain to cause problems in the long run. This is due to the way that eating while we're distracted by concentrating on something else (especially if the 'something else' is making us feel negatively stressed) will give rise to stress-related digestive problems. Eating when we are tense has the undesirable effect of impeding the process of smooth digestion. As a result, if we make a habit of it we are likely to be aware of unpleasant sensations of acid indigestion, heartburn, abdominal bloating and excess gas on a frequent or intermittent basis. This is obviously going to do very little to make us feel on the ball and focused during a demanding afternoon's work.
- Make the effort to reverse this negative trend by making sure that you take some proper time out at lunch. This needn't involve a three-course meal that takes a few hours, but it does need to

involve getting away from your work surroundings, even if it's only for half an hour. By getting away from the building in which we work, we are giving ourselves the chance of a walk in the fresh air (which is in itself relaxing). While eating, make a point of consciously letting go of any obvious areas of tension, and always avoid quickly gulping down poorly-chewed mouthfuls of food. The best way of guarding against this is to avoid reading, watching television or being involved in anything that serves as a distraction while eating. By making a point of relaxing while we eat, we are certainly going to enjoy the eating experience more fully, while also giving our digestive systems the best chance of working so smoothly that we are unaware that it is happening.

- Try to make a point of eating something small every couple of hours in order to keep your blood sugar levels stable. This is of particular importance when we are under pressure at work, since unstable, fluctuating blood sugar levels can give rise to a number of subtle, distracting symptoms that can compromise our overall performance. These can include lack of concentration, mood swings, dizziness, lack of mental focus and irritability. Bearing this in mind, if we are faced with especially demanding pressures at work, it makes an awful lot of sense to keep our blood sugar levels as stable as possible so that we can perform as well as possible. As we have already seen in the section above that considers the merits and demerits of snacking on sugary foods and drinks, we know that the best way of keeping blood sugar levels as stable as possible involves staying away from snacks that include a lot of refined (white) sugar. Instead, we should aim to have a piece of fruit, rice cakes, a piece of wholemeal bread with a savoury topping or a handful of unsalted nuts every couple of hours or so.

- Don't forget to drink regular quantities of water each day, ideally choosing the filtered variety or still mineral water. Too much carbonated mineral water can contribute to feeling rather bloated and gassy during the day. Drinking at least five large glasses of water a day is to be especially recommended for anyone who works in surroundings that are not air-conditioned in summer, or that are heated to very high temperatures in winter. Taking regular drinks of water becomes an even greater priority if we do a job that's physically demanding in over-heated surroundings.

- If morning tends to be a very rushed affair with little time for breakfast, it is well worth making the effort to get up half an hour or so earlier in order to have something to eat. This is especially important if we have noticed that we have a tendency to roll out of bed, grab a quick cup of coffee and a pastry as we're running out of the door, only to discover that we are flagging by mid-morning. We can positively reverse this negative trend by ensuring that we have enough unrefined, complex carbohydrate at breakfast (possibly combined with a small helping of protein in order to give ourselves a bit of extra staying power). The ideal breakfast to help us achieve this effect would consist of a wholegrain cereal (home-made muesli, ideally soaked overnight in order to break down the starches and make it more digestible, is perfect). This could be followed by a round or two of wholemeal toast with a small amount of organic honey or preserve. Alternatively, if we prefer a savoury option on some mornings, we could have a poached or scrambled egg on wholemeal toast.

Options to avoid (since they're going to make us feel stodgy and bloated rather than raring to go at the start of the day) include fried bacon, egg and sausage, lots of heavily-sugared refined cereals, or fat and sugar-filled pastries or doughnuts. For extra zing, try a cup of refreshing green tea or a weak cup of china tea with a slice of lemon.

Chapter Seven

Alternative Solutions to Common Stress-related Problems

It helps to remember that, apart from all of the broad-ranging positive strategies we've considered so far in managing stress in the workplace, we have also got an important avenue of essential support at our disposal in the form of alternative and complementary medicines.

Although for well-established, chronic stress-related problems we would be best to consult a trained alternative or complementary practitioner in order to allow the most positive results to emerge from treatment, self-help can also play an important role in helping us to deal with the symptoms of negative stress. Some of the most common problems are discussed below, with general suggestions being made for a broad range of alternative self-help troubleshooting strategies that can help us get back on top form again.

Should we find that any of these measures help a great deal, but only in the short-term because our symptoms keep relapsing, this would suggest that our problems are very treatable by alternative/complementary means. In this case the help of a trained practitioner is required in order to get the temporary improvement to hold.

You may discover that you want to know more about the background and history of some of the complementary therapies mentioned below as you become more familiar with their practical application. You will find a reading list at the back of this book that will point you in the direction of some general, introductory titles on the theory and practice of some popular complementary therapies. These have been deliberately chosen with the beginner in mind, so that they avoid unnecessary jargon and theorizing, and provide a wealth of practical information that will help broaden your practical, working knowledge of the therapies that interest you.

Effective Self-help from Aromatherapy, Homoeopathy and Herbalism for some Common Acute Stress related Problems

Tension and Cluster Headaches

These are some of the most common problems that can be triggered by a build-up of negative stress levels. Rather than seeing them purely as a nuisance to be got rid of and ignored as quickly as possible, it can be genuinely helpful to see persistent, recurring problems such as tension headaches from a contrasting perspective that may empower us to deal with them more effectively and decisively. Any symptom that keeps on coming back after temporary suppression through painkillers can be seen as one of the persuasive tools our bodies have at their disposal to communicate to us that all is not well.

In this way, recurrent headaches can be seen as the equivalent of a warning light on the dashboard of a car that will come on and draw our attention to something that needs attending to. If we continually ignore this signal, we are sure to have bigger problems further down the line. Our bodies tend to respond in the same way if we continually ignore recurrent symptoms that must to be addressed if we want to enjoy optimum health and vitality.

As a result, it makes a great deal of sense if we're having problems with frequent headaches to try to identify any common triggers that can make us vulnerable to developing these symptoms. The most common are:

- lack of sleep
- over-indulgence in food and alcohol (or an unfortunate mixture of both when we're over-tired)
- postural problems
- muscular tension in the head, neck, shoulders and upper and lower back
- erratic blood sugar levels
- emotional or mental stress
- fighting an infection with an associated high fever.

It also helps to identify the specific sort of headache we tend to suffer from, since this can help us decide what course of treatment is going to be most helpful in easing the pain or preventing the problem from developing in the first place. The most common types of headache include the following.

'Morning After' Headaches

'Morning after' headaches tend to be self-explanatory since they most often occur as a result of drinking excessive amounts of alcohol, or indulging in an unwise mixture of alcohol such as beer, wine and spirits. They are sometimes referred to as a vascular headaches because of the widening and relaxing effect that alcohol can have on blood vessels.

Vascular Headaches

Vascular headaches are identified by the amount of dilation (widening) involved of the blood vessels to the head and neck. This can happen independently of taking any alcohol.

Migraines

Migraines embrace a much more intense experience than we expect from the average headache as, apart from extreme pain, the whole body can feel affected. Common symptoms include disabling headache, nausea, vomiting, visual disturbance that may include zig-zagging peripheral vision or flashing lights, a general feeling of 'toxicity' in the system, disorientation, difficulty in accessing words, and possible tingling of the lips, face, extremities or down one complete side of the body.

Cluster Headaches

Cluster headaches tend to involve one-sided pain that occurs on a sporadic basis. The intensity of this pain can be considerable, with the discomfort waking the sufferer from sleep. In addition, the eye and nostril on the affected side may water for as long as the pain persists. It is in the nature of cluster headaches to last for a few hours, to come and go sporadically over a few days, or to disappear for months at a time.

Tension Headaches

These can often be directly traced to tension in the muscles of the scalp, jaw, face, neck and shoulders. They can be set off or aggravated by postural problems.

General Practical Self-help

Strange as it may sound, if recurrent headaches have set in as a problem, we should avoid over-relying on painkillers as a way of managing the situation. Although taking the odd, infrequent dose of a painkiller can be an appropriate way of dulling a distressing headache, there are distinct disadvantages that follow automatically reaching for the bottle of painkillers at the first suggestion of a twinge of pain. The possible problems that can come from routine use of painkillers include rebound pain when drug is withdrawn, digestive symptoms such as nausea and constipation, dizziness, and possible signs of psychological as well as physiological dependence.

In addition, it is worth bearing in mind that a significant amount of attention has been focused on the need to strictly monitor the use of paracetamol, due to the possibility of liver damage occurring if the dose is accidentally exceeded. Above all else, care should be taken when using powerful codeine and paracetamol formulas, since although these are powerfully effective pain relievers, they can cause a significant amount of drowsiness and can trigger severe constipation. In addition, codeine needs to be treated with a great deal of care, since it can be associated with 'rebound' pain that can occur every few days. Instead of taking this type of preparation on a regular or routine basis, it is worth moving to a paracetamol-only formula taken strictly within the recommendations of the suggested dosage. Once this has been accomplished it may be possible to find an alternative or complementary way of treating the pain that avoids dependence on conventional analgesics.

- It is a good idea to steer clear of any foods or drinks which we suspect may trigger or aggravate our headache symptoms. Common culprits include alcohol (especially red wine and gin), cheese, chocolate and strong coffee. All of these have a particularly strong negative reputation for being common triggers of migraines. For some practical suggestions of how to replace some of these items with healthy alternatives, see the previous chapter.
- Guard against dehydration by drinking roughly eight large glasses of filtered water a day. This is of particular importance to regular headache sufferers, since low-grade dehydration can leave us vulnerable to regular headaches.

- Make a point of trying to enjoy a regular, restful pattern of sleep, especially when stress levels are high. This can be an important factor in discouraging tension headaches or migraines that are related to an overly-pressured or demanding lifestyle.

Check that conditions at work aren't contributing to problems with recurrent tension headaches. These can be aggravated by regularly hunching over a badly lit desk and/or by sitting in a chair that doesn't comfortably support your back in an upright position. Also check that you haven't developed a common habit of leaning to one side while cradling the telephone receiver against a lifted shoulder and ear. Lighting should also be considered, since flickering or fluorescent lights can cause particular problems for those of us who are no strangers to the misery of migraines by triggering off visual disturbance (which is the first sign of an acute episode in classic migraine sufferers). An ideal lighting system should be bright enough to enable us to see quickly, accurately and sharply, but not so harsh that it puts strain on our eyes.

- Tension and stress-related migraines and headaches may be eased considerably by taking relaxation techniques on board. These could include learning meditation techniques or attending a yoga class. The latter has the dual benefit of making us familiar with postures that condition and relax the body, while learning calming and re-balancing breathing exercises.
- If we strongly suspect that postural problems are making migraines or recurrent tension headaches worse, it is time to consider having a few sessions of the Alexander technique. Although not strictly a relaxation or exercise therapy, the basic principles of the technique can be invaluable in pointing out to us the negative postural habits we may be adopting that can contribute to problems with recurrent tension headaches and/or migraines.

Aromatherapy
The pain of tension headaches and migraines may be soothed by applying one drop of peppermint essential oil onto a cottonwool bud and rubbing it gently along the hairline at the front of the head (where it meets the scalp). Alternatively, if you find the smell appealing and invigorating, two drops of peppermint essential oil

can be dropped onto a tissue or handkerchief and inhaled. If you have especially sensitive skin, make sure the essential oil is held at least one inch away from the tip of the nose so that it doesn't make direct contact with the skin.

Headaches that are worse premenstrually or during a period may respond to applying two drops of clary sage essential oil onto a cottonwool bud and rubbing it along the margin of the forehead and the hairline.

Soaking in a soothing bath scented with a few drops of lavender and clary sage can be immensely relaxing to those of us who suffer from tension headaches at the end of a busy, demanding day. To make this soothing aromatic blend, add five drops of clary sage with the same amount of lavender essential oil and mix with two teaspoonfuls of sweet almond as a base oil. Add the fragrant mixture to a warm, rather than very hot, bath. Menstruating women should restrict the use of clary sage to the day before the period is about to start and the first day of the flow, taking care not to over-use clary sage during a period.

Herbal Help
If we prefer to use a herbal soak to unwind at the end of a stressful day, we can choose to combine soothing, calming herbs that can help dispel tension headaches with an oatmeal base. The latter will have the additional desirable effect of conditioning any patches of dry, irritated skin that we may have (this can often arise in winter due to being exposed to a combination of cold temperatures out of doors and drying central heating indoors). To make the preparation, add one cup of bran or fine oatmeal to three cups of camomile or dried lime flowers. Decant the mixture into a muslin bag and suspend in the warm bath water. If you have any doubts about your skin reacting to any of the herbs, it is a good idea to stay in the bath only for a few minutes at first, rather than having a long soak.

An infusion of limeflower, valerian or lemon verbena can ease the pain of a tension headache or a migraine. In order to make the infusion, one cup of boiling water should be added to a teaspoonful of dried herb. Infuse for 15 to 20 minutes, strain, and sip as a soothing, warm drink.

Taking feverfew is thought to be an effective way of preventing the onset of migraine headaches. A fresh leaf can be taken between a couple of slices of bread once a day as a simple preventative measure.

A cup of meadowsweet tea can soothe away cluster headaches due to the aspirin-type compounds that are to be found in the flowers and leaves. A cup of the tea may be taken up to three times a day to ease pain and discomfort.

Homoeopathic Help
Homoeopathic remedies are available through most pharmacies and some healthcare outlets. Symptoms that can be treated this way are detailed below.

Throbbing Headaches
Throbbing headaches that are made worse by the slightest movement may effectively be eased by a few doses of Bryonia, especially if the following symptoms are also present:

- a headache brought on or aggravated by low-grade dehydration
- migraines or headaches that are associated with constipation, with a total absence of urge to 'go'
- terribly sensitive scalp with the headache being aggravated by the slightest, light touch to the top of the head
- pain that begins above the left eye and radiates to the base of the skull.

Left-sided Migraines that Come on after Sleep.
This type of pain may be eased by Lachesis (a homoeopathic remedy made from the highly diluted venom of the surukuku snake, which is particularly useful for the treatment of premenstrual sleep problems), especially if any of the following symptoms are also present:

- bursting, congested pains that extend from the left eye to the side of the nose, or that move from the left to the right side of the head
- dizziness and disorientation with pain that is made more intense by closing the eyes
- severe headaches that are brought on by over-exposure to sunshine or intense heat, or premenstrual headaches or migraines that lift almost as soon as the flow begins.

Tension Headaches or Migraines Induced by Alcohol or Prescription Drugs

Tension headaches or migraines that are brought about by an excess of alcohol and over-reliance on prescription drugs almost always respond positively to Nux vomica, especially if any of the following symptoms are also present:

- classic 'morning after' headaches with heavy sensation at the back of the head and a strong desire to be left in peace and quiet to sleep it off
- recurring waves of nausea with headache and constipation, with lots of fruitless urging to no productive end
- headaches that follow a period of 'living in the fast lane' with a proportional lack of restful sleep, and taking refuge in too much coffee, junk food, alcohol and cigarettes in an effort to try to maintain the pace.

Cluster Headaches With Marked Dizziness and Nausea

Cluster headaches that are accompanied by dizziness and nausea can benefit from treatment with a few doses of Pulsatilla, especially if the following symptoms are also present;

- Right-sided headaches with pulsating pains and burning discharge from the eye on the painful side
- Severe dizziness and nausea with headaches which are all made much worse for being in stuffy, over-heated, poorly-ventilated surroundings
- Headaches feel better for gentle exercise in the open air.

Indigestion and Other Stress-related Digestive Problems

Indigestion is something that we are all likely to experience from time to time, usually as a result of eating something that disagrees with us or simply eating too fast. However, should we begin to suffer the twinges of indigestion and general digestive discomfort on a frequent or long-term basis, it is time to consider whether we have a problem with stress management. This is because our digestive system tends to react very negatively to any excess of negative stress and pressure.

If we think back to the first chapter of this book where we explored the links between the 'fight or flight' response and the reaction of the digestive system, we can imagine that triggering this stress response on a regular basis is almost certainly going to have a significant negative impact on the well-being of our digestive tracts. Common stress-related digestive symptoms include regular or intermittent bouts of indigestion, lack of appetite, griping pains in the stomach or abdomen, acid washing into the throat, excess gas, bloating, diarrhoea and/or constipation. As we can see, too much badly managed stress does our digestive system equilibrium absolutely no good at all!

Common factors that can trigger regular digestive discomfort include any of the following:

- anxiety, nervousness or depression
- smoking (thought to irritate the stomach lining)
- being overweight (this can contribute to problems with hiatus hernia)
- drinking too much strong coffee
- regular intake of alcohol (especially spirits)
- a high-fat diet (tends to put more stress on the digestive tract as fats take more time and effort to be broken down and digested)
- chewing food too quickly
- certain foods that have a reputation for setting off or aggravating symptoms of indigestion, including raw onion, cabbage, pulses, sprouts, beans and cucumbers.

It is important to point out that although an infrequent bout of indigestion that is related to an obvious cause is nothing to be concerned about, recurrent episodes of problems of this kind should not be overlooked. If any changes occur in digestive functioning, such as frequent episodes of digestive discomfort or marked change in bowel movements that can't be linked to any obvious cause, this should be mentioned to your GP.

General Practical Self-help
There are many simple ways in which we can help ourselves to prevent aggravating our digestive system, as detailed below.

- It makes a great deal of sense while under stress to avoid any foods that you may know have a tendency to aggravate problems with indigestion. Depending on each individual situation, these may include any of the following: spicy foods, full-fat dairy products such as cheese and cream, red meat, and deep fried or battered foods. Instead, choose items that are soothing and easily digested (which also tend to be generally healthier into the bargain), such as home-made soups, lightly-cooked (steamed or stir-fried) dishes, salads, non-citrus fruit, pasta, wholegrain rice and small portions of fish or chicken (ideally from an organic source).

- When life is fraught it is especially important to make a point of chewing food thoroughly, rather than relying on gulping something down while we're on the run. It helps to remember that the process of digestion begins in the mouth, since this allows saliva to lubricate the ground-up food, making it easier to swallow as well as allowing for digestive enzymes to get to work. Because this makes the job easier for the stomach, we can readily imagine how bolting inadequately chewed food is very likely going to contribute to problems with excess gas and a sense of heaviness and acidity in the stomach.

- Make a point of eating small meals at regular intervals rather than relying on large, heavy meals that are separated by long gaps. It helps to be especially aware of this tendency during phases of high stress and tension, since these are the very times we may be tempted to skip meals and gulp down snacks while we're working. Missing regular meals and making a habit of snatching the odd bag of crisps, chocolate bar or muffin tends to be equally counterproductive as far as smooth digestion goes. This is due to the combination of problems that stem from inadequately chewed food and the accumulation of bloating, gas and discomfort that can be aggravated by unreasonably long gaps between meals.

- Strange as it sounds, it's wise to avoid relying on antacids to manage indigestion and acidity in the stomach. Although these appear to ease the discomfort of indigestion fairly immediately, they can cause more problems in the long run. These problems are linked to something called acid rebound, which is triggered when our bodies register that stomach acid levels have been reduced (by the antacid). This encourages further secretion of stomach acid in order to rectify the balance of stomach secretions, and so we're effectively back where we started. It's also worth bearing in mind that products using a bicarbonate of soda base can have an adverse effect on symptoms of water retention and high blood pressure, while aluminium-based antacid gels can aggravate symptoms of constipation.

- Always try to avoid eating when feeling uptight, tense or upset because this can directly aggravate or intensify symptoms of indigestion. Instead, if something irritating or upsetting has happened, make a point of breathing steadily and slowly for a few minutes in order to relax and diffuse tension levels. Once you've taken a moment to relax, then consider eating.
- If indigestion is a problem generally, it helps to steer clear of combinations of food that have a reputation for making digestion more of a challenge. These can include red meat combined with potatoes, followed by sweet pastry or full-fat foods such as cheese with bread or biscuits. For more detailed advice on food combining, it would be sensible to explore the principles of the Hay Diet.

Aromatherapy
Make a soothing aromatic massage oil that can be rubbed on the area just below the rib cage in smooth, gentle, circular movements. Add two drops each of mandarin, ginger, peppermint, black pepper and Roman camomile essential oils to two teaspoonfuls of carrier oil. However, avoid this blend if you are suffering from indigestion or heartburn in pregnancy.

Herbal Help
Sipping an infusion of fennel, peppermint, camomile or lemon balm can help bring up wind and ease digestive discomfort. These can be bought in convenient tea bags that simply need boiling water added to them and left to infuse before pouring. Alternatively, one teaspoonful of the dried herb can be used for each cup of boiling water. Measure the required amount into a warmed teapot and leave to stand for 15 minutes before straining.

Taking a warm milky drink to which slippery elm bark has been added has a terrifically soothing effect on irritated stomach linings. Mix a teaspoonful of the powder with a little cold milk or water to form a smooth paste before adding the rest of a cup of warmed milk, stirring all of the time in order to prevent lumps from forming. If the taste of the basic slippery elm formula is too bland you may prefer to try the flavoured variety instead.

Adding spices to food that have a reputation for soothing the stomach and aiding digestion can be helpful. These include cumin, coriander, fenugreek and cayenne.

Homoeopathic Help
Indigestion Due to Over-indulgence
Nux vomica should be the first port of call for indigestion that follows a general phase of over-indulgence, especially if several of the following symptoms are also present:

- queasy, stress-related headaches that feel like a classic hangover (with pain that radiates from the back of the head to the eyes)
- constipation with lots of fruitless urging, but with little result being obtained
- irritability, impatience and mental and emotional 'shortfuse'
- poor sleep pattern with an inability to switch off and get into a refreshing depth of sleep
- craving for coffee, alcohol and cigarettes in order to maintain the pace (these all have a counterproductive effect, making the discomfort of indigestion worse).

Indigestion due to Rich or Fatty Foods
Queasiness and heaviness in the stomach that have been sparked off by an over-rich meal may be eased by Pulsatilla if the majority of the following symptoms are also present:

- a dry mouth without any perceptible thirst
- 'repeating' of food eaten a few hours earlier
- stomach pains and discomfort that are very sensitive to jarring or sudden jolting movements
- tendency for all symptoms to be eased by gentle exercise in the fresh air and to be aggravated by sitting in stuffy, over-heated surroundings.

Indigestion Triggered by Anticipatory Anxiety or 'Nerves'
Stress-related digestive discomfort that seems to always come on

when thinking about an upcoming stressful event such as giving an important presentation at work may be eased considerably by a dose of two of Lycopodium. Choice of this remedy would be confirmed by the presence of a high proportion of any of the following symptoms:

- lots of loud rumbling and gurgling in the belly and abdomen
- digestive discomfort and bloating made more intense and uncomfortable by a tight waistband (this sensitivity is likely to progress in intensity as the day goes on)
- classic heartburn symptoms (pain and burning with acid fluid washing up into the throat from time to time)
- severe and persistent flatulence and gas that may choose to move in an upward to downward direction (or, if we're especially unlucky both ways at once).

Burning Indigestion and Acidity
Sometimes we find that burning indigestion and acidity can be soothed by sips of warm drinks. When this situation develops within the context of a lot of background anxiety (especially in hard-driven perfectionist personalities), the homoeopathic remedy Arsenicum album may be helpful. This is definitely worth a try if the following symptoms are also present:

- a general anxiety about the possibility of serious health problems emerging when symptoms are present
- restless and terrible chilliness with digestive upsets such as nausea and diarrhoea
- most digestive discomfort is worse during the night, with attendant problems in switching off and sleeping soundly.

Severe Indigestion with Trapped Wind
When most of the discomfort of indigestion can be traced back to problems associated to a build-up of gas, the homoeopathic remedy Carbo veg can act almost as if by magic. The choice of this remedy would be confirmed by the presence of the following symptoms:

- violent or persistent burping with corresponding bloating of the waist and belly
- gassy feelings and discomfort that are made much worse by

having anything to eat, however small
- digestive uneasiness and nausea that are made much more severe by being deprived of fresh air and are relieved by being near a cool fan or sitting in close proximity to an open window
- heavy, full sensation in the stomach with indigestion.

Fatigue and Burn-out

If stress-induced physical, mental and emotional fatigue continue unchecked for too long, we are at risk of burn-out. The good news is that finding practical strategies for combating persistent fatigue can do an enormous amount to prevent the more serious and disabling problem of burn-out from setting in.

Common symptoms of fatigue can be broad-ranging in their nature and may include any of the following:

- poor concentration and ability to focus on mental tasks
- lowered or absent libido
- poor digestion with lack of appetite
- cravings for sugary or salty foods
- fleeting or severe muscle aches and pains
- headaches
- erratic mood swings.

An experience of recurring or severe fatigue is one of the surest signals our bodies can send us to tell us that we need to address some problems in order to get our bodies back on track again. More often than not, any combination of the following can be responsible for symptoms of fatigue appearing:

- a phase of extended or severe stress at work and/or at home that may not have been managed adequately or well
- 'burning the candle at both ends' by working too hard and playing too hard for too long
- relying too much on junk foods at the expense of nutritional status
- lack of enjoyable exercise
- relying on too much coffee and alcohol to maintain the pace and wind down

- poor relaxation skills
- lack of refreshing, regular, good-quality sleep
- becoming too involved and immersed in highly-competitive sports or forms of exercise, where the need to win has taken over from the pleasure of the physical experience.

General Practical Self-help

Explore forms of exercise and movement that have a reputation for energy balancing: these can stimulate extra energy when we need it, or encourage us to wind down when chilling out. Ideal systems of physical activity to consider include yoga, t'ai chi or Pilates. These have the added benefit that they are totally non-competitive, allowing each person to fulfil their own potential as and when greater skills develop (and not before!). Yoga and t'ai chi teachers also place a great deal of emphasis on the important role that body awareness plays in helping us to relax through use of simple, but effective breathing techniques. As a result of this gentle, holistic approach to integrating mind and body, stress-induced injuries are much less likely to be a problem.

Above all else, avoid the tendency to reach for 'quick fix' foods when feeling stressed out and 'running on empty' as far as energy levels go. As we have already seen in the section on keeping blood sugar levels stable in the previous chapter, sweet foods and caffeine (two of the usual quick-fix suspects) will only give us an injection of energy in the short term. As a result, it is really a form of false help that only serves to trigger bigger problems in the energy stakes further down the line. Follow the guidelines already given for foods and drinks that give us the maximum chance of slow-release, consistent energy levels. Try as far as possible to avoid any items that give us hefty portions of refined (white) sugar, salt, caffeine and hydrogenated fats, these are most commonly found in margarines, ice-creams, cakes, cheese spreads, biscuits and some forms of milk or white chocolate.

Be vigilant about keeping well within your weekly alcohol allowance, especially when the pressure is on, since this can be a common time when we may be more vulnerable to that extra drink or two in order to help us wind down and relax. Sadly, we will be subverting ourselves if we choose to take this route, since alcohol has an adverse effect on sleep patterns when taken on a habitual basis, and can make us feel pretty wretched on waking. This is partly due to the fact that we have a reduced chance of deep, refreshing sleep after too much alcohol, and partly due to the dehydrating effect that alcohol has on our bodies (not to mention the additional strain it puts on our livers). If you do have the odd night out and want to have the best chance of waking feeling at least semi-human, always make sure that you have a large drink of water before retiring, and keep drinking water during the course of the next day. Since alcohol also has a reputation for depleting vitamin C in the body, make a point of having lots of fresh fruit and vegetables for a few days. Particularly rich sources include kiwi fruit, strawberries, blueberries, peppers, tomatoes, dark green vegetables and Brussels sprouts.

Make a priority of taking time out to relax. This could involve anything that is especially appealing that has nothing to do with work. It needn't involve anything more ambitious that taking a long soak in a warm bath each night, ideally having added a few drops of calming essential oils to the bathwater first. Take time out each night to unwind with a novel, go to the cinema, relax with friends, or cook if you find it therapeutic. The most important thing is to choose an activity that suits your personality well. If following a formal relaxation or meditation programme suits you, that's fine, but don't feel confined to something that's formally organized. Following your instinct should be an invaluable way of discovering what is going to help you unwind best.

Aromatherapy
Short-term mental fatigue and fuzzy-headedness can be rapidly lifted by vaporizing a few drops of stimulating, motivating essential oils such as eucalyptus, rosemary, grapefruit or peppermint. Alternatively, if you don't have access to a custom-made vaporizer, you can place a drop or two of any of these essential oils onto a tissue or handkerchief and inhale as often as required. Take care to keep the tissue at least one inch away from contact with your nose, especially if you suffer from very sensitive, reactive skin.

Flower Essences
Elm may be helpful for those of us who have a tendency to take on an excessive workload, only to find that we feel quickly become

overwhelmed by the resulting responsibility involved in getting through the volume of work.

Beech may be more helpful in situations where perfectionist tendencies lead to an intolerance of faults in others as well as in ourselves. As a result, we may be using up a profound amount of energy in feeling constantly on a short fuse with others and the mistakes we perceive them to be making.

Herbal Help
Wild oats, ginseng or vervain may be taken in tincture, capsule or infusion to act as a nervous restorative.

If a depletion of nervous energy is causing problems with digestion, it may be helpful to take a calming preparation of valerian in short courses. Long-term courses should be avoided, as valerian can trigger headaches, palpitations or muscle spasms.

Helpful Dietary Supplements
Co-enzyme Q10 has been christened 'the spark of life' due to the capacity it appears to have for stimulating flagging levels of energy. It appears to be especially helpful in re-establishing an increased sense of vitality if we have just come through a particularly stressful patch in life. Since it can be rather difficult to ingest quantities that are high enough to have a therapeutic effect by relying on diet alone (around 30 mgs a day), we would do well to consider supplementing with this nutrient for a month or so. Doing this will allow our bodies to get back on track once again. To gain maximum benefit, of course, we also need to get our diets and sleep patterns sorted out rather than relying on taking this supplement alone.

Homoeopathic Help
The symptoms that can be relieved by the use of homoeopathic remedies are detailed below.

Fatigue Due to Unaccustomed Exercise
If you are a couch potato and have headed to the gym or the step class full of the best intentions, only to find that you're crippled with aches and pains and exhaustion the following day, a few doses of Arnica can be just what's needed. Additional symptoms that suggest that this remedy is needed can include any of the following:

- generalized muscular aching, tenderness and restlessness
- sore, bruised feelings that seem to cover the whole body on even the slightest movement – it may even hurt to urinate!
- extreme physical tiredness with restlessness
- extreme consciousness of muscular discomfort at night: whatever surface is lain on feels too hard.

Physical Exhaustion Due to Mental Strain and Anxiety
The homoeopathic remedy Lycopodium can be immensely helpful in getting those of us back on track who have terrific mental drive, but feel in poor physical condition. As a result, we may often find ourselves in a position where we plan to do things but seldom carry them out. Additional symptoms that suggest Lycopodium may be helpful can include any of the following:

- anxiety and digestive problems that tend to come very much to the fore when under pressure
- a lot of mental and emotional distress can be triggered by a sense of control being threatened. As a result, long-term, erratic changes to a previously established routine can result in a build-up of mental and physical exhaustion
- a tendency to poor muscle tone and development, but development of a strong commitment and determination once the decision is made to get physically fit
- extremely, irritability, criticism of others and general crankiness when stressed out.

Physical, Mental and Emotional Burn-out
For those of us who have pushed ourselves to the limit under pressure, Nux vomica can be immensely helpful in giving us the support we need to break an ultimately destructive cycle of living in the fast lane for too long. The presence of a significant number of the following symptoms would suggest that Nux vomica is definitely worth considering:

- competitive instincts that may have got out of control, resulting in an inability to switch off physically and mentally and a tendency to work into the night, making it really difficult to re-establish a healthy, refreshing sleep pattern

- caffeine addiction may become a significant problem because of the need to keep going for punishingly long hours under pressure.
- digestive problems include persistent indigestion and stubborn constipation. These can be brought on or made worse by drinking excessive amounts of alcohol, smoking and possibly relying on painkillers (especially codeine formulas) to deal with tension headaches or to unwind
- constant headaches of a 'hung over' nature, with pain often being located at the back of the head, radiating to the forehead
- because of a considerable competitive nature, a tendency to become addicted to punishing exercise programmes (partly as a result of the challenge and partly due to the endorphin rush that follows regular aerobic exercise).

Physical Collapse Following a Period of Extreme Nervous Energy and Anxiety

For those who suffer physical collapse, Arsenicum album can be very effective in restoring mental and physical resilience – for example when, exhaustion has occurred in perfectionists after meeting a punishing deadline. If a significant proportion of any of the following symptoms are present, this is certainly a remedy worth considering:

- extreme physical and mental restlessness with very high levels of anxiety about being able to meet demandingly high standards
- a tendency to push oneself beyond reasonable work limits and goals, resulting in profound exhaustion
- possible exercise addiction as a result of subtle addictive tendencies and a base-line desire for being as much in control as possible. When this sense of control is threatened profound anxiety can be the result
- compulsion to neatness and order this continues even when someone is too exhausted to leave their bed since they are likely to go on being bothered by any disorder around them
- physical, mental and emotional exhaustion in as a result of a regularly disturbed sleep pattern with an irritating, persistent tendency to wake in the early hours of the morning feeling agitated.

Although all of us are likely to feel fluctuations in mood from time to time (either in response to an external trigger or a more internal cause such as shifts in hormonal balance), provided these fluctuations don't linger, they should not be a matter of too much concern.

However, if problems hit us at the least opportune time, or if they seem to mount up until we feel overwhelmed and we happen to be at a low physical ebb, we may be vulnerable to a more severe situation setting in. If we are concerned that we may be a potential candidate for this sort of problem with regard to established mood swings, it helps to be aware of the most common triggers that can set off negative or erratic changes in frame of mind. They may include any of the following:

- sleep deprivation that continues for an extended period
- temporary suspension of a generally healthy diet
- a stressful atmosphere at work and/or at home
- an extra or unexpected stress load with an non-negotiable immediate deadline
- drinking an excessive amount of alcohol
- relying on too many sugary foods in the diet to keep going
- drinking too much caffeine on a regular basis
- recovering from a nasty viral illness, such as flu
- phases of sharp fluctuations in hormone levels (for example, at ovulation, pre-menstrually or menopause)
- feeling socially isolated
- experiencing lack of satisfaction at work.

General Practical Self-help

If mood swings are creeping up as a regular occurrence, it's time to take a long, hard look at the amount of potentially addictive substances you may be taking on a regular basis. Items to consider include sugar, caffeine, chocolate or other stimulants including guarana, and painkillers that contain codeine and caffeine. If you take all or most of these on a regular or daily basis, there is a considerable chance that they will be contributing to the presence of moderate or marked mood swings. If you suspect that this is the case, eliminate the offending substances slowly and steadily, rather than attempting to do so at once, which would be a shock to your system.

Create some space within which you can cut yourself some mental slack; this should be a particular priority if we find that our mood swings are instantly provoked by the smallest of things. By taking some time to practise progressive muscular relaxation, guided visualization or meditation exercises, we will be allowing our mind the vital opportunity to switch off and replenish themselves. As a result, mood swings should become less of a pressing issue.

As we've already seen, unstable blood sugar levels can also contribute significantly to changes of mood. By taking practical steps to do as much as we can to keep blood sugar levels balanced, we will be taking a proactive step that our mental health is likely to thank us for. For practical advice on how to set about this successfully, see the relevant section in the previous chapter.

Don't forget about the vitally important role that aerobic exercise can play in positively balancing mood. This is due to the way that regular aerobic activity stimulates the production of endorphins (natural antidepressants that are produced by the body, which also have pain-relieving properties). It is the increased secretion of these naturally-occurring chemicals that is responsible for the natural 'high' that follows a period of sustained activity. Always bear in mind that it is most important to aim for regularity when exercising in order to gain maximum benefit from your chosen activity, avoiding the temptation to be over-ambitious when setting goals for ourselves. Ideally, aim for half an hour of aerobic activity engaged in three or four times a week, making sure above all else that the activity you choose in enjoyable and fun (or you can be sure you'll be tempted to give up at the first hurdle).

Aromatherapy
Decant three or four drops of clary sage, lavender, ylang-ylang or sandalwood essential oils into a warm bath the choice may be determined by the aromas you find most appealing. Let the oils float on top of the water after the bath has been run and soak for as long as it feels soothing, uplifting and pleasurable.

Herbal Help
If we need help in cutting down on some of the addictive substances listed above, taking diluted tincture of wild oats daily can help detox the system, while also reducing any symptoms of nervous exhaustion.

Take eight drops of the tincture diluted in a small glass of water each day for a month.

Tense, uptight moods can be soothed by sipping a cup of lemon verbena. It can also reduce the discomfort of a nagging headache that may have been brought on by feeling stressed.

Homoeopathic Help
Some symptoms that respond well to homoeopathic remedies are detailed below.

Mood Swings That Veer Between Feeling Irritable and Fed Up
Feeling mentally, emotionally and physically drained can indicate that the homoeopathic remedy Sepia may be helpful. Although often prescribed for women at times of hormonal upheaval (premenstrual, during and following pregnancy, or at menopause), it can also be a useful remedy in treating males, provided that enough symptoms fit. Major characteristics that Sepia may help to relieve include any of the following:

- extreme feelings of indifference in those who are normally extremely focused and dynamic
- diminished or absent libido as a result of feeling overloaded with negative stress and responsibility
- emotional, mental and physical exhaustion which can be temporarily perked up by engaging in aerobic exercise
- mood swings that are made noticeably worse by plummeting blood sugar levels

Volatile Mood Swings Aggravated or Triggered by Surges in Hormone Levels
Lachesis is always worth considering in situations where highly-creative people find that their volatile streak is becoming a burden. Women in particular can benefit from this remedy if they suffer from severe mood swings premenstrually, but as with the previous remedy, this does not prevent men from also responding well at times of stress. Additional characteristics that Lachesis can help to relieve include:

- abrupt mood swings that can move rapidly from feeling 'high' and on top of the world to feeling despondent

- negative changes in mood which are likely to be aggravated by a disturbed sleep pattern . This may be so severe that someone delays going to bed due to a fear of lying awake for hours on end
- anxiety may be a particularly strong symptom with corresponding problems of palpitations, muscular tension, aches and pains. Symptoms tend to be more intense on the left side, or limited to this side of the body
- all symptoms tend to be worse on waking with mood being especially low at this time
- sleep pattern is likely to be restless, with lots of vivid dreams and a tendency for the limbs to twitch when drifting off to sleep.

Mood Swings Due to Too Much Stress and Too Little Sleep
Those of us who have been using negative coping strategies to deal with an escalating stress load (such as depending on junk food, caffeine, alcohol and cigarettes to hold things together), with resulting problems with concentration, focus and mental and emotional well-being, should consider taking Nux vomica for a few days. This will effectively provide support by improving sleep patterns, and helping the body detox while we get our lives back in order. The choice of this remedy would be confirmed if some of the following characteristics are present:

- marked irritability with a tendency to snap at the least provocation
- mood swings that are most noticeable and severe at the start of the day, and tend to improve as the day goes on
- extremely disturbed and poor quality sleep patterns due to a high intake of caffeine (in the form of regular cups of strong coffee, cola-type drinks and tea) is also likely to trigger palpitations, muscular tightness, aches and pains, and a general inability to switch off and mentally and physically rest
- a general sense of feeling 'hyper' and on constant 'red alert' that may have got to the stage of undermining rather than enhancing productivity and efficiency.

Neck and Shoulder Pain

As we have already seen in the headache section, pain and discomfort in the neck and shoulders is almost always symptomatic of a high negative stress load. The good news is that we have various practical ways of helping ease and manage the situation, but for this to work we must first acknowledge that a problem exists. Should neck, shoulder or back pain emerge, always avoid the common trap of taking constant doses of increasingly strong painkillers or anti-inflammatories in the hope that it will just go away. Unless you're experiencing pain as a direct consequence of a muscle strain that you can identify as resulting from a specific incident where you may have overdone things, the chances are that the situation needs an alternative sort of management in order to resolve a growing problem.

General Practical Self-help

One of the best ways of dealing with chronic neck and shoulder tension is to invest in a neck and shoulder massage once a week, or as regularly as we can commit to the sessions. By benefiting from a hands-on approach of this kind, we can ensure that tense, knotted muscles are slowly and gently coaxed to relax. As a result, blood supply to the head is likely to flow more efficiently and we are far less likely to suffer from regular tension headaches. Regular massage treatment is also one of the most relaxing therapies we can enjoy, so when stress levels are especially high it's time to head for the massage table!

If you are aware that postural habits are contributing to regular aches and pains in the neck and shoulder, the Alexander technique may be an invaluable help in showing you how to learn and benefit from new, more positive postural habits. As we gain in familiarity with this technique, we are likely to be amazed at how physical our response to negative stress can be. And what's more, we are also likely to be amazed at how this response is centred around tightening up the muscles of our neck and upper body without our consciously realizing it. Alexander technique teachers are trained to show us how to identify these negative postural habits so that we can learn new, positive ones. Believe me, as I know from personal experience, this can involve a fascinating voyage of self-discovery.

Try this simple tip to relieve tension in the jaw and facial muscles (where an awful lot of neck and shoulder tension originates). Consciously relax the muscles of your face by closing your eyes and focusing on every area of tension from your forehead downwards. As you concentrate on letting go of any tension around your jaw on either side, you may notice you lips part slightly as you let go of any tension you may be holding in this area. If this feels difficult to do, take the tip of your tongue and gently press it for a second or so against the area where the roof of your mouth meets your top teeth. Once your face feels fully relaxed, breathe out and consciously let your shoulders drop an inch or two away from your ears. Finally shake out your arms and hands to relax any tension; this is especially helpful for anyone who uses a VDU workstation all day.

For further suggestions on self-help alternative and complementary therapies that may be useful, see the section on tension and cluster headaches.

Eye Strain

Those us who work at computer terminals each day are at particular risk of low-grade eye strain without realizing that there may be a problem. Common symptoms of eye strain may include:

- squinting and furrowing up the forehead on a regular basis
- regular low-grade headaches for no other apparent reason
- sore, dry eyes.

General Practical Self-help
If you suspect that you may be suffering from eye strain, the first helpful practical step is to consult an optician, especially if you are suffering from recurrent headaches. It may be that you now require reading glasses, which can happen almost routinely for anyone over the age of 50, or if you already wear glasses for work, it may be that your current prescription needs adjusting. Opticians can also be very helpful in picking up early signs of additional problems that may be developing, such as high blood pressure, glaucoma or cataracts. We should also make a point of having regular check-ups at our opticians if we suffer from diabetes, since opticians have sophisticated equipment at their disposal to check for any complications that can arise affecting the eyes (such as diabetic retinopathy).

One of the most important and simple ways of guarding against eye strain becoming a problem is to ensure that we blink at frequent intervals. As obvious as it may sound, it is amazing how many of us can become so absorbed in concentrating on a piece of work that we stare at a document or a VDU screen unblinkingly. This can have the undesirable effect of making our eyes feel strained and tired. In order to avoid falling into this trap, get into the habit of blinking at regular intervals, rather than relying solely on automatic reflex.

If your eyes feel tired, try a technique called 'palming'. All it involves is gently placing the cupped palms of your hands over each eye socket while keeping your eyes closed. For an extra-relaxing effect, you can rub the palms of your hands together vigorously so that they feel extra warm. Sit back, relax, and keep your hands in this position while you do a few calming breaths.

There are several jobs that are inherently stressful – air traffic control, police, teaching and so on – and people going into these professions should recognize this and choose differently if their personality type is unable to cope with stress. Health and well-being is paramount; without this you cannot perform efficiently in your job or profession. Therefore, if work changes and lifestyle changes don't reduce your stress, it is worth considering changing the job (different company or different type of work) rather than endangering your health.

Recommended Reading

Benson, Herbert, *The Relaxation Response* (Collins, 1976)

Benson, Herbert, *Beyond The Relaxation Response* (Collins, 1985)

Campsie, Jane, *De-Stress* (Murdoch, 2000)

Grant, Doris and Joice, Jean, *Food Combining For Health – The Original Hay Diet* (Thorsons, 1984)

Guiffre, Kenneth, *The Care and Feeding of Your Brain*: How Diet and Environment Affect What You Think and Feel (Career Press, 1999)

Kenton, Leslie, *10 Day De-stress Plan: Make Stress Work For You* (Random House, 1994)

MacEoin, Beth, *Anxiety and Depression* (Wellhouse, 2001)

MacEoin, Beth, *The Total De-Stress Plan: A Complete Guide to Working With Positive And Negative Stress* (Carlton, 2002)

Pearson, Philip, *Keeping Well At Work* (Kogan Page, 2001)

Pfeiffer, Vera, *Stress Management* (Thorsons, 2001)

Rushton, AnnA, *Stress* (Wellhouse, 2004)

Selby, Anna, *Home Health Sanctuary: Weekend Plans to Detox, Relax and Energise* (Hamlyn, 2000)

Smith, Tom, *Depression* (Wellhouse, 2002)

Sullivan, Karen, *Panic Attacks* (Wellhouse, 2002)

Viagas, Belinda Grant, *Stress: Restoring Balance to Our Lives* (Women's Press, 2000)

Vyas, Bharti with Haggard, Claire, *Beauty Wisdom: The Secret of Looking Good and Feeling Fabulous* (Thorsons, 1997)

Wilson, Paul, *Calm At Work* (Penguin, 1998)

Useful Addresses

Aromatherapy Consortium

PO Box 6522
Desborough, Kettering
Northamptonshire NN14 2YX
Tel: 0870 7743477
www.aromatherapy-regulation.org.uk

British Acupuncture Council

63 Jeddo Road
London W12 9HQ
Tel: 020 8735 0400
www. acupuncture.org.uk

British Massage Council

17 Rymers Lane
Oxford OX4 3JU
Tel: 01865 774123

Society of Teachers of the Alexander Technique

1st Floor, Luton House
39-51 Highgate Road
London NW5 1RS
Tel: 0845 230 7828
www.stat.org.uk

National Institute of Medical Herbalists

56 Longbrooke Street
Exeter EX4 4HA
Tel: 01392 4260622
www.nimh.org.uk

The Society of Homoeopaths

11 Brockfield
Duncan Close
Moulton Park
Northampton NN3 6WC
Tel: 0845 450 6611
www.homoeopathy-soh.org

MIND/National Association for Mental Health

Granta House
15–19 Broadway
London E15 4BQ
Tel: 020 8519 2122 or 020 8522 1725
www.mind.org.uk

Transcendental Meditation

24 Linhope Street
London NW1 6HT
Tel: 0207 402 3451
www.t-m.org.uk

The Institute of Optimum Nutrition

13 Blades Court
Deodar Road
London SW15 2NU
Tel: 020 8877 9993
www.ion.ac.uk

The Nutri Centre

The Hale Clinic
7 Park Crescent
London W13 1PF
Tel: 020 7436 5122
   www.nutricentre.com

British Wheel of Yoga

25 Jermyn Street
Boston Road
Sleaford
Lincolnshire NG34 7RU
Tel: 01529 306851
www.bwy.org.uk

Other titles available from

Wellhouse Publishing

HOW TO COPE SUCCESSFULLY WITH

ANXIETY AND DEPRESSION

Beth MacEoin

We live in stressful times and have to cope on a daily basis with a variety of different pressures. These can include financial worries, emotional stresses, bereavement, break-up of relationships and insecurity at work. When feeling well and resilient we are able to cope with a wide range of these stressful situations. It is when we become mentally and emotionally overloaded at a vulnerable time in our lives that we can suffer from symptoms of anxiety or depression. Beth MacEoin describes in her easily accessible style the various symptoms and suggests a wide range of practical measures to provide positive support.

ISBN: 1-903784-03-4   128pp

CANDIDA THE DRUG-FREE WAY

Jo Dunbar

Candida is the common name for an overgrowth of yeast organism known as *Candida Albicans*. Candida appears with many seemingly unrelated symptoms − it affects almost every part of the body and has become an umbrella term for any collection of symptoms of no identified cause. Because of the wide range of symptoms and the lack of positive diagnostic tests available, this gap has provided fertile ground for individuals of limited medical training to quickly hop on the band wagon and begin 'diagnosing' Candida for almost any condition or illness. This book introduces a thorough drug-free treatment program, as well as tips on how to adapt your life-style to treating Candida.

ISBN: 1-903784-11-5

128pp

COLITIS

Dr Tom Smith

We know a lot about the changes that occur in the bowel of people with colitis and how to return them to normal. It should be only a matter of time before we know *why* these changes happen. Colitis means 'inflammation of the large bowel' (the colon), inflammation takes several forms and doctors have different views from the general public on what constitutes colitis. Most of this book is devoted to ulcerative colitis and Crohn's, with chapters on how to distinguish these inflammatory bowel diseases from irritable bowel, diverticular disease and colon cancer.

ISBN: 1-903784-12-3

128pp

CROHN'S DISEASE

DrTom Smith

Although on Crohn's disease, this book compares the similarities and differences to ulcerative colitis. Dr Smith describes how modern medicine is used to relieve and prevent serious complications. He explains how the normal bowel works, how it can go wrong and why it can produce the three main symptoms of diarrhoea, bleeding and mucus. This book describes the tests, investigations, and the diagnosis of the illness. It is not just the illness but how much of the bowel is infected that affects the treatment and how quickly and completely recovery is made. Other bowel problems that mimic Crohn's are described.

ISBN: 1 903784 16 6   112pp

DEPRESSION

DrTom Smith

In his easily accessible style DrTom Smith describes depression and explains why we get depressed, the treatment with drugs together with other treatments. It shows how to think through your depression, what you can do for yourself and how to change those negative thoughts, become more outward going and assertive together with sleep problems. Depression is a serious illness that needs serious attention. Everyone in the family doctor's team has to help, the sufferer's family must also be aware of the risks and how to give assistance. DrTom Smith describes in this book the help you can get.

ISBN: 1903784 14 X   112pp

DIABETES

Dr Tom Smith

If there was ever a role model for people with diabetes, insulin-dependent or otherwise, Sir Stephen Redgrave is it. Few people with diabetes aspire to his Olympic gold medal heights but everyone can take heart from the way he put his body through the most rigorous training and still kept good control of his diabetes. The main aim of this book is to achieve a good quality of life despite the health hiccup of diabetes. This book describes all aspects of the healthy lifestyle that every person with diabetes needs to follow, it is positive and optimistic to give people with diabetes a sense that they can shape their own future.

ISBN: 1-903784-02-6

128pp

DIVERTICULITIS

Dr Joan McClelland

Diverticulitis is a Cinderella disorder. It is very common, can be dangerous and there are rapidly increasing numbers of sufferers. We stand a more than 50 per cent chance of suffering from diverticulitis before we reach the age of 60. Dr Joan McClelland describes in her easily accessible style the symptoms, different types of diverticulitis, complications and various treatments including alternative and herbal remedies. This book also covers the psychological aspects of diverticulitis and the benefits of exercise and diet.

ISBN: 1-903784-00-X

128pp

HIGH BLOOD PRESSURE

Dr Duncan Dymond

Blood Pressure is not a disease, everyone has a pressure, we need it to keep us upright and alive. Your blood pressure varies depending on your level of physical and mental stress. In this easily accessible book Dr Dymond describes what high blood pressure is, the symptoms, various medications available, side effects and possible complications. The tests and investigations for high blood pressure are explained together with treatments and suggestions for changes to lifestyle and diet.

ISBN: 1-903784-07-7   128pp

HIGH CHOLESTEROL

Dr Tom Smith

We are all becoming more aware of high cholesterol problems and often only discover that we are at risk when having a geneneral health check. In this book Dr Tom Smith describes in his easily accessible style the causes of high cholesterol, the associated problems, the complications and the risks involved if your high cholesterol goes untreated. Dr Tom Smith details the treatments available together with possible side effects. He also gives information on diet and lifestyle changes which may be needed to help reduce your cholesterol levels and reduce the risks to your overall health.

ISBN: 1-903784-09-3   128pp

HOW TO COPE SUCCESSFULLY WITH

IRRITABLE BOWEL SYNDROME

Richard Emerson

Irritable Bowel Syndrome is a complex problem with both physical and psychological symptoms. The aim of this book is to set out clearly and concisely these symptoms and the various treatments now available – conventional, complementary and alternative. Ths should enable sufferers to improve their lifestyle and either cure or manage their Irritable Bowel Syndrome.

ISBN: 1-903784-06-9

128pp

HOW TO COPE SUCCESSFULLY WITH

MENOPAUSE

Dr Joan McClelland

The menopause is an event to welcome, a stimulating new chapter in your life. You can say goodbye to period pains, water retention, PMS together with a host of psychological problems including irritability, depression and chronic tension. The menopause is a vantage point from which to take stock, reviewing your earlier life and looking ahead to new interests, deepening relationships and fresh goals. You are entering an important and fascinating time in your life and to get the best out of it you need to work in harmony with nature, this book aims to help you achieve this aim.

ISBN: 1-903784-05-0

128pp

HOW TO COPE SUCCESSFULLY WITH

MIGRAINE – THE DRUG FREE WAY

Sue Dyson

Imagine someone is trying to drill a hole through one of your eyes, your stomach is heaving. your sight disturbed by weird effects of light and shade – and pins and needles in your fingers and toes. Sufferers will recognise some of these symptoms. This book is for anyone who feels that conventional medicine isn't the whole answer. It looks at the dietary components that bedevil many migraine sufferers' lives. It's not just about cheese. red wine and chocolate – but complex patterns of food intolerances and sensitivities. Identify these and real improvements can be achieved.

ISBN: 1 903784 17 4   128pp

HOW TO COPE SUCCESSFULLY WITH

PANIC ATTACKS

Karen Sullivan

Panic attacks are a much more common problem than is generally realised an affect a large proportion of the population. They can manifest themselves in many ways including agoraphobia, anticipatory anxiety, separation anxiety, school or work phobia. This book explains what Panic Attacks are, the causes, how panic affects daily life and the associated disorders. Conventional treatments together with their side effects are explained and alternative remedies including acupuncture, homoeopathy, reflexology, massage are covered. Karen Sullivan gives reassuring short term measures to help deal with an attack and, together with other advice, Top Ten Tips to help cope in the longer term.

ISBN: 1-903784-08-5   128pp

SLEEPING WELL – THE DRUG FREE WAY

Beth MacEoin

Good sleep is an important part of your total health. There is no uniform pattern to sleep problems, a great deal depends on an individual's make-up. Problems include difficulties in switching off, frequent waking and a sense of being unrefreshed on waking. Other factors may be over-reliance on caffeine, alcohol or chemical sedatives. Bad working habits can play a large part in preventing sound sleep. This book contains positive strategies to solve these problems and break the negative cycle. The major systems of alternative medicine included in this book have a different perspective to conventional medicine on the issue of sleep problems.

ISBN: 1 903784 13 1   128pp

STRESS

Anna Rushton

Stress is about change and how we deal with it when we live in a society where there are many changes happening in rapid succession. In this accessible book AnnA Rushton describes Stress. explains the chemical changes that happen to your body and shows how to identify signs of Stress including a Stress assessment chart. AnnA describes what professional help is available and explains what self-help options there are including: Diet & Nutrition, Exercise, Lifestyle Changes, Stress Management, Relaxation Time, Alternative Therapy guide plus Top Tips to handle your Stress.

ISBN: 1 903784-18-2   128pp

HOW TO COPE SUCCESSFULLY WITH

THYROID PROBLEMS

Dr Tom Smith

The thyroid is not a subject that immediately springs to mind when we chat socially about our health. We marvel how some people have boundless energy while others are always tired and weary. There are nervous, anxious, agitated people who can never sit still. It is easy to assume that people differ in these ways because of their characters or lifestyle but a substantial number have developed these characteristics through no fault of their own. These are the sufferers from thyroid problems. Do Tom Smith describes in his easily accessible style the symptoms, different types of thyroid problems, complications and the various treatments available today.

ISBN: 1-903784-01-8   128pp

HOW TO COPE SUCCESSFULLY WITH

YOUR LIFESTYLE DIET

Karen Sullivan

A healthy diet is more than just balancing food intake, it involves eating foods that promote rather than endanger health. What are the elements of a healthy balanced diet? How do we identify which are good fats, bad fats and essential fats? What problems can be caused by sugar in our diet? What are the different types of sugars found in our diet and which are healthy? What should we drink and what should we avoid drinking? What essential supplements do we need? The answers to these questions and many more are contained in Your Lifestyle Diet.

ISBN: 1-903784-04-2   128pp

NO DIET WEIGHT LOSS

Pat Walder

- Have you tried of an endless variety of diets?
- Do you find you lose some weight, then put it all back on again – plus a little more?
- Do you envy those people who can eat whatever they like and never put on weight?
- If you answered yes to any, or all, of the above questions, then what is contained within the pages **No Diet Weight Loss** will solve all your problems. This is a radical new way of achieving your perfect body weight and maintaining that weight PERMANENTLY – without diets, pills, potions or excessive exercise.

Dr Tom Smith said about this book:-

'This book is full of common sense and good advice on how to change one's life permanently to overcome all the habits that produce obesity. I will certainly recommend it to my patients. It gives people an excellent insight into themselves and how they have become overweight. It gives rational and sound advice on how to change their attitudes and lifestyle, not just so that they can be thinner, but happier with themselves, too. And it does this in a style that is easy to read, with humour and sympathy. An excellent book for everyone involved in obesity – and nowadays that means more than half of the adult population. I wish I had written it myself.'

ISBN 1-903784-10-7

88pp + CD